THE BUSINESS ADMINISTRATION
OF A CHURCH

THE BUSINESS
ADMINISTRATION
OF A CHURCH

BY

ROBERT CASHMAN

Business Manager of
The Chicago Theological Seminary

HARPER & BROTHERS

PUBLISHERS · NEW YORK

THE BUSINESS ADMINISTRATION OF A CHURCH

D-Y

Dedicated to

WILLIAM H. LEACH

Editor of *Church Management,* and pioneer in better business administration for the churches of America. As preacher, writer, counselor and personal friend, his life has been an inspiration to ministers and laymen throughout the land.

CONTENTS

Does the Church Need Business Management? 1

I. The Minister's Office 5

II. Files and Records 11

III. Correspondence 23

IV. Church Organization 32

V. Advertising and Publicity 44

VI. Church Finance 56

VII. Christian Stewardship 68

VIII. The Sexton 74

IX. The Use of Time 84

X. Personal Conduct 92

XI. The Care of Church Property 102

XII. CONVENTIONS, CONFERENCES AND SPECIAL MEET-
    INGS 111

XIII. THE SWINDLING OF MINISTERS 126

XIV. EXECUTIVE LEADERSHIP 144

XV. A MESSAGE TO LAYMEN 156

THE BUSINESS ADMINISTRATION
OF A CHURCH

DOES THE CHURCH NEED BUSINESS MANAGEMENT?

A SUCCESSFUL minister will accept the threefold responsibility of preaching, pastoral service and executive leadership. Many a good sermon has been preached to empty pews and countless faithful pastors have faced discouragement in their work because business management had been neglected, both in personal and in church affairs.

The subject of business administration in religious work is not new, for since men began to build temples and to accumulate property to establish and beautify their houses of worship, the church has been a business institution. One of the greatest burdens of the apostle Paul was the business organization and the financial support of the churches he had established.

Today in America alone there are 212 denominations, with 232,000 churches, each of them a separate business enterprise. These churches have a membership of 45,000,000, and spend every year for their current budgets the sum of $817,000,000. The value of church properties is $3,800,000,000, not including such items as parsonages, schools, hospitals and endowment investments. Thousands of men and women are on the employed staffs of the church, while millions of workers are engaged in various volunteer capacities.

With such staggering responsibilities upon our ministers and the denominational officials who must supervise their work, does it not seem singular that so little business training is given by theological schools in their preparation of the leaders who must bear the burdens of the management of the church?

Some may feel that church administration is the layman's task — and it is, if the minister knows how to delegate it. But it should be remembered that while the church is the first responsibility of the minister, business and other personal vocations may claim the layman's interest and his time.

" It is my observation," says one of the most prominent and successful pastors of the Middle West, " that the ordinary group of laymen in any church, no matter how large and strong it may be, will not carry on efficiently the business of the church without the wise oversight, the brooding care and the inspiration of a practical-minded minister."

Every item in the program of the church is the responsibility of the minister until he can assign it to others. The efficient minister will delegate to his paid staff and volunteer helpers practically all of his business duties, remembering that " it is better to put ten men to work than to do the work of ten men." Having done this, however, even though his organization be complete and functioning perfectly, he will remember that his is a task also of supervision. He will give praise and appreciation to the deserving, encouragement to the disheartened, and instruction to those who may not understand their work.

Ten years ago the Chicago Theological Seminary established a course on the business administration of the church, which included instruction concerning office equipment, filing, correspondence, advertising and publicity, convention management, the care of church property, organization, finance and executive leadership. While the classes were well attended, there was from certain sources immediate opposition to this departure from the beaten path. One prominent layman, in a syndicated editorial which was widely published, said: " We are chaining divinity to a desk. We are asking prophets to serve as presidents of corporations."

Others approved the new course, however, and answered editorially that " while the weight of evidence seems to be against increasing the preacher's responsibilities, there is precedent to the contrary in biblical times: Job, for instance, divided his hours between preaching and producing; Nehemiah spread the gospel while he undertook to rebuild Jerusalem; Daniel found time to rule the provinces of Babylon and to preside as chief of the governors and the wise men while he prophesied and preached." Similar tributes might be paid to Abraham, Joseph, Moses and many others whose religious leadership was strengthened because they were also masters of business administration.

It is scarcely conceivable that, in the larger churches, the minister could be less than a well balanced preacher, pastor and business executive.

Laymen take pride in a good minister. They crave his personal fellowship. They boast of him to their fellow men, and especially to the members of other churches. They invite him to address their business conferences, and they look up to him as a source of strength to their community. And the good minister is one who is master in all three aspects of his work.

While the subjects treated in this book are somewhat elementary, it is my conviction after years of study, with innumerable conferences and an ever growing correspondence of inquiry, that ministers are in need of assistance and instruction along the lines of practical business administration. It is to meet this need that this book is offered.

CHAPTER ONE

THE MINISTER'S OFFICE

WHAT is an office? According to the dictionary, an office is " a place where business is carried on." Is the minister's office only a " place "? Where should it be located? What should be its equipment? Why should there be a church office, or a minister's office? The consideration of these and other related questions will soon reveal to us the importance of establishing an up-to-date office as a " workshop " for the minister and his staff.

Describe your office to me, and I can estimate the value of your business leadership. Is it clean and orderly? Is it arranged to save your time, and that of your constituency? Is it easy to find, cheerful and hopeful in its atmosphere, convenient to the church? What are its good points; its inconveniences? What improvements could make it more effective?

An office may be confined to the corner of a room, or it may occupy a suite of rooms. It is a place for the management of a business, where people come and go, where plans are made, orders issued and records kept. Its size and its equipment are dependent entirely upon the needs of the program to be promoted. A minister's office may be considered the office of the church, and the minister its chief executive.

OFFICE EQUIPMENT

The minimum equipment for such an office might include at least the following:

5

A flat-top desk, with a glass desk pad, lamp, inkstand, pens, pencils, paperweight, ruler, shears, paste, pins, clips, rubber bands, etc., and two filing trays.

A swivel desk chair on ball-bearing casters.

Two side chairs (preferably with arms, but not rockers or easy chairs).

Bookcases, a vertical (four-drawer) steel filing cabinet, and a card file.

A typewriter and desk or stand, also a mimeograph or other duplicating machine.

Telephone, clock and calendar.

Rugs or carpets, and pictures for the walls.

A flat-top desk is preferable to one with a roll top, if for no other reason than as a constant reminder that one's work is not finished until one's desk is cleared. The temptation to use the pigeonholes of a covered desk for miscellaneous filing and to pull down the top over an accumulated pile of unorganized papers is thus removed.

In the selection of a desk, one should exercise care to see that the smaller drawers and their partitions are spaced to receive cards of standard sizes (3 x 5 and 4 x 6 inches), and that the larger drawers are equipped for vertical filing. A filing drawer in the side of the desk with pressboard guides and manila folders is an important aid in organizing one's work. Papers and documents frequently used, such as budgets, minutes, reports, agenda, etc., should be kept near at hand in one's desk rather than in the larger vertical file, which should be placed as close as possible to the desk. The card files likewise should be readily available.

Under the glass desk pad may be kept lists of official boards, telephone numbers frequently used, engagements and dates to be remembered, together with a calendar, a map of the city or of the world, and such charts or other information as may be desired for constant reference.

The position of the desk and of the chairs is important as related to the entrances to the room, light, and the general harmony of the equipment to be used. An executive's desk should " control " the room.

A swivel chair is recommended because it saves steps and time, causes less wear on the rug and floor, and makes it easy to turn from one side of the desk to the other for both office work and interviews.

Bookcases should be placed where both artificial and natural light will make quick reference convenient without strain to the eyes; and if possible, they should be within reach of the minister's chair. Every such item of forethought counts in the saving of time, and time costs more than equipment.

Every minister should use a typewriter, and he should take time to learn the touch system. The typewriter desk or stand should be of such a height that the keyboard will be about even with the elbows. The use of a typewriter is a kindness to one's friends. With practice, one learns to write much faster than by hand, and more legibly; carbon copies may be kept for reference; publicity and reports may be prepared without the risk of errors; dockets, budgets, minutes and other official documents may be made attractive. In short, the whole program of church work will take on a more businesslike appearance.

A vertical filing cabinet is almost a necessity. Sermons, correspondence, maps, charts, reports, dockets, minutes, catalogues, programs, printed matter, photographs and other valuable materials may be filed quickly under convenient classifications and proper headings for future use. If I were to organize a minister's materials for a four-drawer steel filing cabinet, I should use one drawer for correspondence, one for sermons, one for subject matter, and one for stationery, printed forms and miscellaneous supplies.

IMPORTANCE OF PICTURES

The pictures on the walls are important. They help to create " atmosphere " both for the minister and for his guests. In the reception room of the Chicago Theological Seminary hang the portraits of the twenty-four directors, and certain historical scenes depicting both denominational and institutional development.

In my own office I have pictures of leading officials and of prominent pastors, of cathedrals and local views, a map of the world, and several exhibits from foreign countries. In my pictures there is a point of contact for almost every visitor who comes to see me. I have also many relics and curios from lands across the seas.

A church office should be easy to reach. If possible, it should be near the street and have attractive signs to guide the stranger. Its position relative to entering the chancel should be considered. Lights should be placed in dark passageways and over the entrance door at night. Steps and stairways should be avoided as much as possible. It is a well known fact that a store is less desirable from a rental standpoint if one must go up a flight of stairs to reach it, but we often forget this principle in planning entrances to our churches. If steps must be used in a church or office entrance, it is better if they are placed inside the vestibule rather than outside. If they are already built on the outside, a strong handrail should be installed for use in stormy weather.

The color scheme of one's office is important. There are bright, cheerful tints, dignified tones, and gloomy hues. Walls, rugs, draperies and office equipment — all should harmonize to make an agreeable, restful atmosphere.

The question is often asked: " Shall the minister's office be used by the organizations of the church, such as Sunday school classes, Boy Scouts, etc.? " For governing boards and officials the answer would be " yes "; for subordinate organizations, " no." The minister's office should be recognized as a place of dignity, authority and respect.

ATMOSPHERE

The difference between a minister's office and a business office is largely one of atmosphere. What message does yours give out to those who come for help?

It is said that a disorderly desk is the sign of a disorderly mind. The desks of many ministers are piled high with unanswered letters, loose papers and magazines, books and other unanalyzed and unassimilated materials. Coats, hats and packages are placed on a convenient chair and must be moved for the first visitor who arrives. Tables and shelves are likewise covered. Some people feel that they cannot get into the spirit of their work without having such disorder around them. It is a pernicious attitude. A successful administrator who is to control the forces at his command must first of all put his own house in order.

Ministers should not spend too much time in their offices, but their hours should be regular, not only for the planning of their work, but for interviews which will be sought by their constituencies. Two hours a day, set aside definitely for administrative duties, are better than twice as many in a carelessly organized schedule.

Shall we protect ourselves from interruptions? No. Welcome every caller. Study the revised methods of business executives. Time was when they were " in conference," or " out of the city," fortified by private secretaries. Now they are out in front where they can meet the public, for every human contact is helpful to their interests. I have often felt that if I could only get enough people into the habit of coming to my office I might be called " a success." I would not need to go out for business.

The multitudes will seek you and find you if you make it a point to render " service plus." More good sermons have been forged on the anvil of daily human contacts than ever came from books.

It would be beneficial for ministers to visit the modern offices of successful businessmen, and to compare them with the offices of the church. A study of office furniture and office supply catalogues is also recommended.

A well equipped, smoothly running church office not only will save much of the minister's time and strength, but will become a powerful help in the business administration of the church.

Chapter Two

FILES AND RECORDS

W HERE do you file your sermons? " I asked a minister of one of the largest churches in a Middle Western state.

" In the wastebasket," he replied.

" Why? " was my next question.

" To keep fresh," he answered.

It was no surprise to me a few months later to learn that he had suffered a nervous breakdown from his work.

Probably no profession is more greatly in need of good filing systems and equipment than is that of the ministry. To the minister who would conserve time and strength, the subject of filing is as important as any other feature of his work. Yet it is doubtless true that no executive is more careless than the average minister in the filing of materials which may be not only of inestimable value to him and his associates, but to his successors and to the historical records of the church.

What a gold mine of wealth would be ours if, upon entering a new pastorate, we could find complete and accurate records of the work of our predecessors. Instead, most of us patiently and laboriously must make up our membership and organization lists, gather together such information as may be available, and hope that our statistics are correct.

The question, then, that we should ask ourselves is, " What are *we* doing to build up the foundational records so necessary to ourselves and to those who will follow us? "

VARIETY OF FILES

The first file that most of us can remember was rather simple. It consisted of a stick, or spindle. We see it even today in banks, meat markets and grocery stores, making jagged holes through our checks and bills of sale. It preserves everything, but does not classify it for future use. Such a file does not belong in a minister's office.

Then followed the box file, with its alphabetical division sheets fastened securely at the side. Though simple in design many of these files are still in use. They are recommended as bill (invoice) files, or wherever the material to be preserved does not exceed the facilities of the box.

Next came the flat file, based on the same plan as the box file, except that the contents were in drawers, usually nine to a sectional case, units of which were placed against the wall. The combination of drawers allowed for further alphabetical divisions and for subject files. One drawer might be labeled " Finance "; another " Sermons "; etc. This file was unpopular and did not endure. It was too bulky for its contents. It collected dust and it was not convenient for quick reference.

At last there appeared the vertical file, at first of wood, and then of steel; and this file, we believe, has come to stay. The wooden file gave way to steel because of the former's fire hazard, and because in damp weather the drawers were inclined to jam.

A study of filing cabinet catalogues reveals a wealth of offerings. There are two-drawer files of desk height; three-drawer files of counter height; standard files of four- and also five-drawer design; likewise, safes, supply cabinets, compartments for desk drawers; card, map and document files; small desk files, newspaper files and other excellent equipment for almost every need.

Card files have passed through changes as rapidly as have letter files. A generation ago we were accustomed to files for cards of odd sizes that made it difficult, if not impossible, to transfer a group of cards from one file to another. Today we find boxes, drawers and cases of fiber, wood and steel for cards of standard sizes — 3 x 5, 4 x 6, and 5 x 8 — with alphabetical, numerical, geographical and other guides that discourage every error in filing.

PLANS FOR FILING

Often I am asked for an ideal plan of filing. I have none to recommend. It all depends upon a minister's needs, his habits of thinking and his methods of working. What would fit one office would handicap another. I believe in keeping filing equipment as one's servant rather than as one's master. The first rule would be to keep the system simple and to expand it only as there is need.

The real test of any filing system is this: Can we find what we need when we need it, the relative costs of time and equipment also being considered?

What materials should be filed? At least the following:

Correspondence and telegrams.
Form letters and promotional material.
Catalogues (educational and supply).
Dockets, minutes and reports.
Bulletins, programs and publicity.
Maps, charts, photographs and half-tones (cuts).

Bills, receipts and canceled checks.

Historical, financial and other data.

Lists (or card records) of active and prospective church members, alphabetically and geographically; and by families, age groups, organizations or such other divisions as will be of assistance in one's work.

Baptisms, weddings and funerals.

Sheet music and choir supplies.

Sermons and addresses, both completed and in preparation.

It is better to file daily, or regularly, than to wait for a convenient time. Such a time rarely comes. Do not save worthless or " miscellaneous " material. If it cannot be classified at once as of value, it is needless to save it. Use the wastebasket freely. Clear all files for action.

METHODS OF FILING

As to methods of filing, correspondence may fall naturally into three classes:

(1) *Alphabetical.* File vertically in alphabetical manila folders, in a regular box, desk or cabinet drawer, according to the name of the writer or the firm.

(2) *Subject.* Here the subject of the letter takes precedence over the name of the writer. Perhaps the subject is evangelism, preaching missions, financial campaign or a new building. Put all correspondence relating to each subject in a separate folder, label, and file in the regular alphabetical drawer. When enough folders have been accumulated to justify it, the subject folders may be removed to a special subject file.

(3) *Chronological.* This system is convenient where a follow-up is desired. Many cases treated by correspondence are incomplete. They cannot be filed away and forgotten. Answers are required. Perhaps we must write several letters before a certain problem can be solved. The other person may forget, but we must not. Label a folder " Post-dated," keep it near at hand, perhaps vertically at the front of the desk filing drawer; combine by pin or clip all correspondence pertaining to the case, attach a covering slip on which is marked the date (at the right-hand corner) for follow-up, and file chronologically. Review this file daily. When a case has been completed, it may be transferred to the regular alphabetical file. Suppose, for instance, that a man writes me and promises one hundred dollars for my work at a date six months from now. How shall I remember to make the collection? I acknowledge his gift, mark the correspondence for attention six months ahead, and file it in my chronological or post-dated file. Such a file " never forgets."

Some filing systems provide for the numbering of subjects, these numbers running consecutively, as from one to one thousand, with one number for a subject; others allowing perhaps ten numbers or certain decimals for a general department, so that the various branches of a given subject may be kept closely together. Such methods are good for accounting, but are not recommended for filing because they require separate indexes or cross-reference cards or other provisions which may become unwieldy, needlessly consume time and thus lose their value.

Form letters and promotional material may be filed vertically and alphabetically in a standard cabinet, by subjects, preferably in a separate drawer; also catalogues, photographs, dockets, minutes, reports and all similar data and supplies.

Many churches have not yet discovered the advantage of filing choir music vertically in steel cases. The old dusty wooden cupboards are still in use. The merit of the vertical file is not only the saving of space and the preservation of the music, but the availability for quick reference and general inventory. A steel cabinet may be moved, but a built-in cupboard must remain in its original location.

In less than three years, the Chicago Theological Seminary has accumulated a library of more than one hundred twenty anthems averaging fifty copies each, all of which are filed vertically in two four-drawer steel cabinets for daily use.

Sermons and addresses may be filed simply and efficiently in open, vertical folders, alphabetically by subject. Such subject folders should include not only all previous addresses given, but should be available, near the minister's desk, for constant reference and the feeding-in of new material. Did you read an item in this morning's paper about " The Futility of War "? Did you clip it, and did you put it in your sermon folder on " War or Peace "? Did you read a new book which contained a message on " The Resurrection "? Will you trust your memory to use this message in your Lenten sermons? Or will you take your note pad and write the subject, the name of the book and the page, and drop the slip into your sermon folder on " The Easter Message " for future reference?

The preparation and the use of such a file are easily mastered, but their possibilities are inexhaustible. In my own work, I have built up a file with more than a thousand subjects, each of them in a separate open folder, yet so simply arranged that a stranger could go to my file and find any subject in my experience. One group of subjects may be in a drawer labeled " Financial "; another " Instruction "; and still another " Addresses." These divisions make reference more convenient.

A survey of the field reveals many other systems of sermon filing, some good and others questionable. Our policy is to pass judgment not on systems or equipment, but rather on the use that is made of them by ministers. If a filing plan serves the needs of certain types of thinking, it is good. If it does not, it may be poor, no matter how elaborate.

THE NUMBER SYSTEM

One distinguished minister and writer files his sermons numerically, with two card indexes — one by topic, which may be listed in as many as six or seven different forms; and the other numerically, in accordance with the folder number containing the sermon. Besides these, he provides a topical file in the office, alphabetically arranged, for the accumulation of new material which is filed by his secretary. Near his own desk, in addition, there is a more personal topical file which he builds up himself. He has also sixty-six folders, one for each book in the Bible, into which he files material frequently; and each of the four Gospels, being considered of major importance, is divided in the file into ten sections, into each of which he feeds material that will be transferred later to his sermon and other files. By this plan, he has collected data on more than a thousand subjects, all filed vertically in open folders.

Another minister files his sermons in large manila clasp envelopes, in the order in which the messages are given. On the outside of each package, at the top, he lists the topic and the text; and below these, at the bottom of the envelope, the illustrations used, these notations being intended for future reference in order to avoid a too frequent repetition of the same material.

Still another pastor files his sermons similarly, but in addition, numbers them and includes on the outside of the envelope the Scripture lesson, the hymns, the size of the congregation, the place, the date of presentation, and his own estimation of the value or success of his delivery. If, for instance, he feels that his message was not well received, he is guided in his preparation, should he repeat the sermon on another occasion. He supplements his sermon file with an alphabetical card index, and includes with the information listed on the cards the numbers of the sermon envelopes.

The only advantage evident in such systems lies in that they enable one to review one's sermons in sequence; while if filed by subjects, such as " Character," " Mothers' Day," " Patriotism," etc., the material would be available immediately for such further use as might be desired. A subject file requires no index unless cross references are desired. A colored sheet of paper may be inserted at the front of the manila folder for this purpose.

Some ministers bind their sermons in book form at the end of the year. This method is good for preservation but not for reference, unless it is supplemented by a card index.

PLANNING AHEAD

Most of us do not plan far enough ahead. All of us ought to outline our sermons at least a year in advance. Practically half our subjects are already set for us. Is it not true, for example, that we shall follow a preaching schedule something like the following?

In September, Labor day, Rally day.

In October, the harvest season, the world-wide missionary program.

In November, Armistice day, Thanksgiving, the day (or week) of prayer.

In December, the every-member-canvass, Christmas.

In January, the message of New Year's, Temperance day.

In February, Father-and-Son week, Lincoln's birthday, Washington's birthday, Vocation day: the call of the Christian ministry.

In March, Education Sunday.

In April, Evangelism and the messages of the Lenten season, Palm Sunday, Easter.

In May, Mothers' day, Memorial day.

In June, Children's day, Baccalaureate day.

In July, Patriotism.

In August, the vacation message.

Here, then, are subjects almost automatically supplied for practically half the morning sermons of the year. In addition to these, which are of universal interest, doubtless each minister can supply half as many more based upon the program of his own church and denomination and upon his attitude to life and the aims of his leadership. That would allow 25 per cent to be determined as the plans and program

of the church develop. The anniversary of the founding of
the church, for instance, could become an important occasion.

If it is as easy as this to determine a year in advance the
general trend of from 75 to 90 per cent of one's sermon topics,
why not start a very simple vertical file containing twelve
monthly guides and fifty-two manila folders, one for each
Sunday of the year? If a minister preaches two sermons on
Sunday, the system would be the same and the number of
folders would be doubled. This plan would apply likewise
to prayer meetings, board meetings and any other regular
sessions of the church.

Let us begin by labeling the monthly guides, " October,"
" November," " December," etc. Then let us enter on the
tabs of the folders the topics, such as " Thanksgiving," " Lincoln's Birthday," " Easter," etc.

What has happened? Like magic, we have turned our
work into play. It becomes a game to see that those fifty-two
folders are filled with helpful material.

First of all, we will look up our old sermons on the subjects we have outlined and will file them in the folders for
review before preparing the next similar messages. We will
add to these the sermons of others on the same subjects, as
we find them. Here is a stimulating article in the evening
newspaper on the situation in China. We will cut it out and
file it in our folder on " Missions." Our magazine clippings
and memoranda sheets will find their places in the right files
from day to day, as will references to helpful passages in the
books which pass before us for review.

As the weeks and months go by, it becomes a pleasure to
look ahead. There is no doubt now, in our minds, as to the
subject for any given Sunday. The folder is filled with ma-

terial and ready for study. October has passed. We may take its material from the beginning of our file and place it at the end, a year ahead. And the same with November and the other months as they come. True, we have preached the sermons indicated, but we have not used all the material.

READY FOR EMERGENCIES

On March 11, perhaps there comes an emergency. Maybe a public disaster occurs. A special appeal must be made from the pulpit. The scheduled sermon cannot be used. What shall be done with it? Put it a year ahead and keep building it up. Or possibly the subject for April 22 has not yet been determined, and this message will fit there just as well.

As a minister begins to develop this plan, he will find himself thinking in terms, not of fifty-two sermons, but of two or three times that many. As he continues his reading and study, there come to him thoughts and sources of material on such subjects as " Love, Its Redemptive Power," " Sin, Its Social Effects," " Humility," etc. What shall he do with these if they do not fit into his sermon schedule for the year? All such surplus material will go into a supplementary subject file.

In the course of time this subject file, likewise, becomes filled with helpful data on perhaps a hundred additional subjects. It is the minister's " meal barrel," his friend in time of need. It takes away his worries. He is ready for any emergency.

Summer comes. It may be the " let-down " season for the congregation, but not for the minister. It is his preparation time for the months ahead. He begins to make up his program for the coming year. He turns to his filing system. Some of his fifty-two folders are transferred to the subject file; others are set forward, perhaps a year. Many of the folders in his subject file take their place in his new sermon schedule. In an almost unbelievably short time he has prepared himself for a year in advance. The contents of his folders show him where he is strong and where he is weak in the accumulation of material. New books must be read on certain subjects, interviews must be sought, and conventions and conferences must be attended for help in completing subject material. The minister sees all this at a glance, and makes it his aim to meet the need.

Vacation time arrives. The minister goes away free from care, and returns rested, refreshed and ready for his work. There is no note of uncertainty in his sermons. Like interest money on one's financial investments, the minister's filing system of sermon material is working for him more than a year ahead of his needs.

Ministers and church workers, train yourselves in methods of good filing! Your requirements may be simple today, but prepare yourselves while there is time. Who knows but that five years from now you may be serving a larger church? Perhaps you may be called to the presidency of an institution, or to an important denominational secretaryship. Will you be ready for such a promotion?

Chapter Three

CORRESPONDENCE

WHEN man began to write letters, he laid another foundation stone for himself in the structure which we call " eternal life."

Among the truly great letters which have lived, we think first of all, perhaps, of the epistles of St. Paul. We may think of others, such as those written by Shelley or Lincoln.

What made these letters great? Was it not their sincerity and their universality of appeal?

" Have you ever *received* a *great* letter? " I asked my class of ministers. " Yes," said one, " I received a message that took me from the farm to college. It changed my whole life." " I received a letter," replied another, " that brought me from a small town to a great city and opened a world of opportunity to me." " And I received one," interrupted a third member of the class, " that gave me the most precious thing I have — my wife."

" Have you ever *written* a *great* letter? " was my next question. Not a hand was raised. Not a word was spoken. I wondered why.

If a letter is " a vehicle containing or conveying our thoughts," why not reach out, as true leaders, and write great letters to our fellow men? The opportunities of letter-writing are unlimited. Letters have been used successfully to increase church attendance, to revive prayer meetings, to enlarge Sunday school classes, to raise money and to collect it, to promote rally days and other special occasions; in fact, to advance the interests of anything where the powers of salesmanship may be applied.   Expert letter-writers can command big salaries, but they must know and use all the elements of successful salesmanship.

KINDS OF LETTERS

There are many kinds of letters, for example:

Informational messages, generally used for educational purposes, preceding campaigns; helpful likewise in cultivating friendships and enlarging one's sphere of influence.

Letters of query.   People like to answer questions, and those who can write letters of inquiry which will bring back the information or cooperation desired have progressed a long way on the road to success.

Inspirational messages, leading to the action desired.

Letters of greeting, appreciation, congratulation, sympathy, comfort or encouragement.   All of these are helpful in making and keeping one's social and business contacts.   The remembrance of anniversaries is always welcomed.

Answers to correspondence from others.   This is what one might call " the daily routine."

Sales or promotional letters.   These are generally mimeographed, multigraphed or printed, and are used for the larger lists of names included in one's organization or constituency.

Successful letter-writing is both an art and a science.   One requires study and practice to reach perfection in it.   It is an educational opportunity, for if one uses new thoughts, words and expressions in his daily correspondence, it is surprising how quickly his vocabulary will be enriched.

Every letter should be answered as carefully as an interview would be conducted. It represents a helpful, human contact. Anonymous letters should never be written, read or answered.

The subject of correspondence divides itself naturally into two parts:

ANSWERING MAIL

First: The answering of mail received from others. Many ministers, educators and other professional men are careless in this respect, forgetting that to keep a friend waiting for the reply to a letter is almost as discourteous as failing to answer the telephone or the doorbell of one's home. All business mail should be answered promptly, and especially that which, if neglected, would delay the progress of others who seek help.

Replying to correspondence gives one not only the opportunity to render the service requested, but to add the influence of one's own life of leadership.

Business letters should be answered the day they are received.

Generally, a reply should not exceed a page in length, and the copy should be so spaced that the margins will be well proportioned, as a picture is in its frame.

Businessmen appreciate it when the subject of the letter is placed at the top of the page, and when a separate letter is written for each subject covered. Otherwise, accurate filing is made difficult.

When writing letters, we should keep in mind the person addressed, rather than our own interests. " You " and " your suggestion " are far more important than " I " and " my idea." If one must be personal, then " we, our committee, our church," etc., are better than " I."

The use of only the right enclosures is important. Some correspondents have the habit of filling an envelope with miscellaneous booklets and pamphlets to the limit that may be carried by its postage. This is a mistake. No enclosure should be used which does not illustrate the subject of the letter. If one is writing on missions, for instance, a missionary leaflet would be the appropriate enclosure.

Church stationery should be white and of standard sizes. The printing should be in black. Abbreviations should be avoided. The names of streets, avenues, etc., should be spelled out in full. A minister's letterhead should be dignified. A small engraving of the church, its tower, entrance or some related emblem may be used to good advantage to make a letterhead attractive. Colored stationery may be used for promotional purposes.

It is always better to express appreciation than criticism in a written message. Many a writer would gladly recall a letter sent in a moment of haste. Avoid the clearing of " misunderstandings " by correspondence. Keep all expressions positive.

Stamped, addressed envelopes should be enclosed if the favor desired is for the writer. " Make it easy for the customer to remit " is a good business slogan for any institution.

Leaders should write more letters than they receive. In addition to answering one's correspondence, a minister will find unlimited opportunities for service to a world-parish. Messages of inquiry, program promotion, commendation and congratulation to missionaries, former parishioners, students at college, denominational officials and fellow workers will bring rich rewards. Spoken words may be forgotten, but letters may live forever.

Second: The writing of sales, or promotional letters. This is far more difficult, and it is in this field that most ministers are untrained and their efforts are likely to fail.

There are many occasions when form letters may be issued profitably by churches, as for the advance promotion of the Every-Member-Canvass, special offerings for benevolent causes, Rally day, membership and loyalty campaigns, the collection of pledges and the announcement of special projects.

A successful sales letter, written for any purpose where cooperation is desired, should include these basic elements:

(1) *The securing of interest or attention.* This may be done in the salutation, as " To you, the Father of a Wonderful Boy," or in the opening paragraph, as demonstrated by a letter recently sent out by an elevator company, which begins: " It would take one man just 83 years and 4 months to learn as much about caring for an elevator as the Otis Maintenance Organization has learned since yesterday morning. Yesterday was 80 years ago." To arouse curiosity as to what is to follow is the first rule of a successful letter.

(2) *The presentation of the general subject or proposition.* When interest has been secured, it is useless to proceed further without clearly stating the object of the message. It would be the same if we were to call on a busy executive. We might greet him with a question about his family, or yesterday's

ball game, but we cannot remain long without giving the reason for our visit. It is not yet time for details, but these follow immediately.

(3) *The separation of the subject into parts, and application of it to the one addressed.* This is the place for facts, analysis, illustrations and proof. It is here that personal desire must be created for the object or purpose to be attained. Suppose, for instance, that we are appealing to a selected list for funds for a church organ. In our first paragraph we might include a question: " Have you ever stopped to think what worship would be without music? " In our second paragraph we could suggest what music, and especially the great hymns, have meant to the church, and how much more enriched our services would be if we only had an organ. In the third paragraph we would present the plan of the music committee to secure such an organ, and we would emphasize the important part that each reader could have in helping to achieve the goal.

(4) *General close.* Just as a salesman must prepare to close an interview, so now the time has come to say good-bye, but we must not do so before we have secured conviction and decision on the reader's part. It is here that we suggest the definite action desired.

(5) *The " clincher."* No sale would be complete without the signing of a contract. The securing of a pledge requires the filling out of a card and its return to a certain person by a given time. Frequently this cooperation can be stimulated by the offer of a reward, as for instance, " If the pledges received by Rally day total two-thirds of the amount desired, we have a friend who will contribute the remainder needed." It is best never to " command " in the close of a letter. The

business house that writes " act now " or the minister who concludes with " send your check by return mail " is making a mistake. Better by far to suggest: " Will you be willing to be one of ten to make possible the sound of joyous music for our children on Rally day? Your early reply will be deeply appreciated."

A postscript is valuable as a " clincher " if its content is stronger than that of the body of the letter. It is best in question form. In a sales letter it should never be used as an " afterthought," lest it detract from the cooperation desired.

A letter of promotion should suggest some definite and worthy action on the part of the recipient. Otherwise it becomes simply a bulletin of information and loses its force. A sales letter should always ask for a reply.

BE NATURAL!

The secret of good letter-writing is to be natural. Think of the person who is to receive the message. Suppose you were to meet him on the street, or to call upon him at his office and talk with him for three minutes — the time it takes to read a letter. What would you say? Would you leave him with a signed pledge in your pocket?

One hundred names are not impersonal. They represent people who have the same interests and emotions as ours. In addressing a form letter to a given list, I sometimes imagine that I have called a meeting of these friends, perhaps in the auditorium or the parlor of the church. I have just three minutes to address them. What shall I say to win their support? My thoughts must be organized and my words must be well chosen. First, I must secure the interest and attention of my audience. Then I must explain the purpose of the meeting, apply my plan to each one who is present, set forth the method of cooperation, and appeal for the action desired. Will I win? If my purpose is worthy, and if the cooperation suggested is definite and within the reach of those addressed, there is every reason to anticipate success. Having made this analysis, I am then ready to write my form letter.

Of course, not every " sale " can be concluded on the first approach. Follow-up letters are sent, just as follow-up calls are made. Business firms sometimes prepare in advance a series of follow-up letters, to be sent at certain intervals, if replies are not received. My own experience in religious work would indicate that where a follow-up is desired, letters may be prepared with more freshness and with greater force if they are based on the results of the previous communications. Suppose, for example, that a series of three letters is required for a certain financial campaign. I may write the first, and outline the trend of the other two; but if I await the early replies to my first letter, I can use the testimonies and other results achieved as fresh material for my second message (and the same with the third), with better results than could be expected if I prepared my follow-up letters in advance.

Form letters have an advantage over personal letters because they allow freedom to make many helpful statements in a general way which perhaps could not be said definitely to individuals without offense. For instance, suppose a campaign is to be launched for church attendance. An individual might be offended at the statement that he had been negligent, but he will take a general appeal in good grace and will offer in return his personal cooperation.

Form letters should be individually addressed and personally signed. If informational, they may be sent by open mail, but if they require any return, and especially that which may pertain to financial help, it is better to send them sealed. Many businessmen do not even open mail which comes to them unsealed.

The best form letters, as well as the strongest advertisements, usually are based upon the development of a single idea.

The leaders in one's organization may be found, instructed, inspired and encouraged by first-hand letters, but the needs of a larger constituency (the followers) may be covered by duplicated forms.

From this day forward, let us become the writers of *great* letters!

CHAPTER FOUR

CHURCH ORGANIZATION

SUCCESSFUL churches are developed not only by strong preaching and faithful pastoral service, but by good organization. Congregations may be aroused and inspired by messages from the pulpit, but they grow in strength and loyalty through service. The largest service is made possible by organization and the assignment of responsibilities. Therefore it is a minister's duty so to arrange his organizational setup that every member of the church is put to work at a definite task.

However, a crowd of people, even with a leader, is not necessarily an organization. It may be a mob.

There were one hundred thousand men and women at a recent music festival in Soldiers' Field in Chicago, but they did not constitute an organization. At almost the same time, there were ten thousand soldiers encamped in Grant park in Chicago, and they represented a perfect organization.

There can be a successful organization only where there is a worthy program moving toward definite goals, and where there is recognized leadership with delegated responsibility. In a volunteer organization, if the program is not worthy both workers and supporters will drop out before the desired objectives are attained.

Having established our goals, the first step is to take inventory of our resources of men, means and equipment. Then we should make plans to use our resources.

THE SERVICE CANVASS

Some churches take an every-member-canvass to discover new talent. It is called a " Service Canvass." Instead of asking for contributions, the solicitors seek service pledges on cards that offer almost every type of practical cooperation in a form somewhat like the following:

I am willing to:
  Become an usher.
  Serve in Scout work.
  Assist in the athletic program.
  Help serve luncheons or dinners.
  Join the home department.
  Care for children in the nursery during church services.
  Teach a class in the Sunday school.
  Play the piano or the organ.
  Act as chaperon, etc.

As many as fifty activities may be listed, so that there is scarcely a person who will not find some item of interest. Such a canvass uncovers a great wealth of volunteer helpers, ready to work; and wise is that church organization which assimilates them while they are interested.

One of America's leading ministers testifies: " I spend many hours every week planning work for my associates."

THE OVERBURDENED MINISTER

Who of us has not heard of the overburdened minister who feels that there is little talent for leadership in his church?

In some churches I have seen ministers rushing around

from the beginning of the children's morning service to the end of the young people's meeting at night, checking details, greeting friends and strangers, and making sure that everything was running smoothly. In other churches I have noted that ministers take the necessary time to find and to train leaders to do these things for them in an orderly and much more attractive way.

If we do the work ourselves, we are criticized; if we get others to do it, we are praised. There is satisfaction as well as glory in personal achievement. It is for the executive to give that satisfaction and that glory to others.

A church program should be analyzed, departmentalized and charted, so that the responsibility of every group may be made clear for purposes of promotion, administration and follow-up. Then committees should be appointed and tasks assigned. To the good workman should be given praise, appreciation and public recognition; to the others, encouragement and assistance, as needed.

The ordinary layman has no adequate conception of the program of the church. He does not know what weekday meetings are held, or what is scheduled for the future. To make all of these details familiar to his congregation, Dr. James W. Fifield, pastor of the First Congregational Church of Los Angeles, California, with a membership of 2,215, publishes a complete official directory of sixty-four pages, in which he gives the history of the church, its present and future programs, a composite calendar of daily proceedings, a list of activities classified under such titles as " Finance," " Administration," " Worship," " Education " and " Extension," showing the names of those who are responsible for the more than two thousand volunteer responsibilities, and giving a complete alphabetical list of church membership with street addresses and telephone numbers. This directory is supplemented by his four-page weekly printed bulletin in which the pastor's personal message and his analysis of current developments in a five-year program are of great value in clarifying the layman's mind and in giving inspiration to the workers to solve their many tasks.

MAGAZINE AIDS

Two of the best magazines known to us on the business administration of the church are *Church Management,* published by William H. Leach, of Cleveland, Ohio; and the *Pastor's Journal,* published by the Board of Home Missions and Church Extension of the Methodist Episcopal Church, Philadelphia, Pennsylvania.

In recent numbers of the *Pastor's Journal,* there have been many excellent messages on church organization. Ministers have not only listed their sermons definitely for a year in advance, but they have charted their churches by diagrams and graphs, and have published their daily, weekly and monthly programs for twelve months ahead. This has been done both by dates and by subjects. Best of all, definite objectives and goals of achievement have been set for the guidance of volunteer workers. For example, the Grace Church Brotherhood of Dayton, Ohio, announces the slogan, " A task for every man, and a man for every task "; then follows its comprehensive program for boys' work, church services, community service, evangelism, finance, social work, stewardship and world service-peace. Under each of these subjects there are from four to eighteen definite suggestions for practical help, and likewise a quota. For example:

Finance Quota
Every person seen during this campaign.
Two hundred special calls on the subject of finance.
Ten seen about their wills.
Project carried through.
Spring campaign finished.

Stewardship Quota
One hundred men tithers.
Present stewardship project.
Fifty personal conferences.
Twenty-five new *Advocate* subscriptions.

Evangelism Quota
Two hundred new members.
Two hundred inactives called on.
Increase average attendance at prayer meeting.
Twenty-five doers each Sunday night from November
   to June.
Fifty men doers actually working.

Such programs, goals and quotas are earnestly commended to other churches.

Another issue of the *Pastor's Journal* contains " A Suggested List of Church Projects or Activities for Use in Preparing a Year's Program for a Church," in which one hundred sixty-four items of service are presented for the consideration of ministers and their congregations, under the general headings of " Worship," " Evangelism," " Religious Education," " Social and Recreational Life," " Finances," " Church Building and Equipment," " Missions," " Family Welfare," " Civic Improvement " and " Cooperation with Other Agencies."

The outline bears the following imprint:

" This list of projects or activities was prepared by the class in social research and field surveys, Drew University, Madison, New Jersey, under the direction of Professor Ralph Felton."

To enlist successfully the help of volunteers, the tasks assigned must be worthy, definite, and within the reach of those to whom they are given.

DANGER OF UNORGANIZED FORCES

Unorganized forces may become dangerous to the interests of the church. Ten good musicians can make a terrible discord. So also can ten trustees, or ten church schoolteachers, or ten good women in the Ladies' Aid Society. I once knew of a men's Bible class that grew so large and strong and independent that it became a menace to the church because the program of the church was not comprehensive enough to include this powerful class.

If opposing forces reveal themselves, usually the best way to deal with them is to enlarge the program of the church and to put them constructively to work. President Díaz did this with a robber chieftain in Mexico. For years a certain mountain pass was a place of danger to every traveler. General Díaz called the chieftain to his palace and gave him a responsible position on his staff. Thereafter, the pass was safe.

In any campaign it is better to overorganize and surpass the goal than to underorganize and fail to reach it.

Let us consider the marvelous organization of one of our larger symphony orchestras. Why is it necessary or desirable to have one hundred instruments playing softly enough to accompany a soprano singer, or a solo on the harp? Why not just a few, playing with more force? Why a dozen first violins and eight bass viols? Would not a fourth as many do as well?

No, the music is sweeter, the tones are more harmonious and the whole effect is more pleasing when each of many instruments is contributing just a little than when a few are trying to do it all. And this also is to be remembered, that power is ever present for use when it is needed. In a symphony orchestra not a single instrument can be spared. It may be that only once or twice in a concert are the flute, the piccolo or the bass drum scheduled for a part, but each must play his part when needed. Should it not be the same in the organization of the church?

KINDS OF ORGANIZATIONS

There are many kinds of organizations to be used for various types of programs. There is the quiet organization which runs smoothly like the hidden wheels of a clock, where only the results are seen. And there is the more dramatic organization which, like the marching of an army with bands and flying colors, creates a feeling of enthusiasm and of confidence in the strength of the machinery itself. The regular program of the church would come under the quiet organization; the special promotional projects might require the dramatic.

Organizations need not only to be set up but supervised until they have reached the goals for which they were established. More than half the organizations of an average church die a natural death before functioning, for lack of supervision and careful follow-up.

I once took part in an important campaign, involving

one hundred men of a leading church, in the course of which calls were to be made on prospective members. The setup was perfect: good publicity, well educated workers, excellent social activities, spiritual emphasis, etc. Then one day the chairman put several hundred record cards on the tables and asked the men to make their own selections of those on whom they wished to call. The minute this happened, I knew that the campaign was over, fruitless, for human nature is such that there must be a follow-up of such assignments, with appreciation and public recognition of work well done. The chairman should have had the cards prepared in duplicate, and in the hands of a list committee who would charge them out to the workers and see that they were followed up within a reasonable time. This campaign was never finished.

Not until the last name has been turned in, accompanied by a definite report, is any campaign completed.

One mistake which is often made in organization is to assign too many tasks to willing workers. A church is never strong, financially or otherwise, whose burdens are carried by the willing few.

Great care should be used in the writing and the preservation of the minutes of all meetings in which actions are taken. The resolutions adopted, rather than the discussions, should be recorded; also the date and place, and a list of the members present. Written reports should be requested from all officers and committees for filing with the minutes.

APPOINTING COMMITTEES

In appointing committees, it is not always best to select only those who agree with us in our policies. Other viewpoints are valuable, even if in opposition to our own, but in business terms, " it is well to keep control of 51 per cent of the stock."

A minister should not act as the chairman of committees, except of those which relate to the spiritual side of the work; and even then, his organization may be stronger and his influence greater if he frees himself from this type of detail.

In one of my courses on the business administration of the church, I received a paper from a Pennsylvania minister, who wrote:

" In our parish, we have one man in charge of publicity. He not only furnishes our news items, but he also clips and catalogues all material that is published. He has several young people working under him who assist in the making of posters, the addressing of letters, mimeographing and other clerical work.

" One person acts as statistician, and keeps all records of church attendance, Sunday school, choirs, and other data such as quarterly financial reports and reports of organizations.

· " In like manner, another layman has charge of finance; one, of property; one, of music; one, of men's activities; one, of women's activities; and one, of benevolent projects. Each person has a subcommittee, and all take part for the joy of the work and for the love of the church.

" Such a setup would mean a great deal of time and labor for the minister, were it not for the help of our most valuable key man, our chief adviser. We are most fortunate to have this man as chairman of the Spiritual Council, and in this capacity he acts. He is a businessman of about fifty years of age, practical and yet a dreamer. His motto is, ' the best for the church.' The pastor shares his ideals, dreams and problems with this man and is in constant touch with him, with the result that the plans of the pastor are translated into action by this minister's business manager without the minister's having to care for the many details which are likely to sap the energy of the man who tries to do everything himself."

Every responsible office should have at least one assistant, for example, an assistant treasurer, choir-director, secretary, church-school superintendent, or whatever the position may require. This provides for a growing organization, and for promotion that may be needed because of illness, removal or transfer of membership. Recently I was asked if it would not be justifiable for a minister to superintend the church school, or to teach a class " in an emergency." I replied that there should not be any emergencies. Good organization would make them unnecessary. As well might the principal of a school become the teacher of a class, or the president of a bank a paying teller. It is the duty of executives to find leaders and to train them for their work, not to do the work themselves.

I believe in having junior deacons, a junior house committee and junior organizations in almost every department of church work. It is the natural way to spread responsibility and to provide new leaders in the course of time. A magnifying of such honors is possible, through worthy installation services at appropriate times. It is helpful to commission the workers in a public service, preceding an every-member-canvass, in order that the tasks may be dignified and that a right attitude may be established before calls are made at the homes of the parish.

Probably less than a fourth of an average congregation is

engaged in any active or constructive service for the church. The other three-fourths are just as talented, but their hidden resources have not been discovered and put to use. Here, then, are almost unlimited opportunities for the minister and his staff.

TEST OF SUCCESS

One's test in business success is often based on how many people one can constructively and profitably put to work. In our business department of the Chicago Theological Seminary, there are not only paid workers, but many volunteer helpers, committees, etc., the same as any minister would find at his disposal in a church. This staff is so well trained and organized that almost anybody could come in and direct it, for a while. In fact, it could carry itself for a while. The real problem of the administrator is in creating new work when the initiative or momentum of the staff gives out, so that each person will be engaged happily in a service that is useful. To keep an organization going is like caring for a clock. Almost any clock will keep good time if someone will wind it and make needed adjustments.

Fortunate is that minister whose staff has enough initiative to cover at least its routine duties without constant supervision.

An executive should organize, deputize and supervise. He should be a coordinator and a lubricator. His work is like that of a gardener, who must plant, transplant, nourish, protect and harvest.

It is unwise in a public service to call for volunteers for tasks to be performed. It is better to pick leaders with peculiar talents to fit the responsibilities at hand. Jesus preached to the multitudes, but he selected his disciples one by one and gave them the challenge, " Follow me." After he had lived with them and worked with them, he was able to say with confidence, " Go ye into all the world and teach."

Having established the policies and the program of the church, and having set up an organization of men and women competent to carry the responsibilities involved, let us trust our associates fully, for they are our partners. Nothing breaks down the morale of an organization more quickly than communication by the head to the individual worker, without recognizing the official staff between.

Happy is the minister who has a committee for every department of business administration, so that with a free mind and a clear conscience he can give the larger portion of his time to preaching, pastoral calling and the other spiritual needs of the church.

Many church programs are too localized. To interest the more influential members of our congregations, we must think of the church as a whole — interdenominational, denominational, world-wide, national, state, conference or association, and finally our own unit, which should be related to the entire organization. An extensive program based on this recognition will have opportunity and responsibility to enlist the cooperation of everybody who is willing to work. In fact, a " Service Canvass " may be required to find additional helpers.

CHAPTER FIVE

ADVERTISING AND PUBLICITY

*Ye are the light of the world. A city that is set on a hill
cannot be hid.*

*Neither do men light a candle and put it under a bushel, but
on a candlestick; and it giveth light unto all that are in the
house.*

*Let your light so shine before men, that they may see your
good works, and glorify your father which is in heaven.*

MATT. 5:14–16

IN THESE three verses of Scripture may be found a wealth
of suggestions relating to advertising and publicity.

There are many ways to advertise, in addition to the use of
the press.

" Church advertising " means making known to the public
that which the minister, officials or committees wish to emphasize. It may be buildings, equipment, program, per-
sonnel or any other special items of church work.

Most of the European cathedrals are built upon the
heights, their towers and spires reaching upward toward the
heavens. Their location commands the countryside in every
direction. Their majesty wins lasting respect. The beauty
and the dignity of their architecture appeal to the religious
nature of passing generations, and call to prayer multitudes
who cannot at all times attend the services within.

Who can imagine a famous castle that was not originally planned with regard to strategic location?

Business firms have recognized the values of right placement, and have spent large sums of money on surveys to be certain that their structures would be seen by the public in a favorable light, and that they would be within the reach of the customers they hoped to attract. They have installed beacon lights, bells, clocks, gardens, rest-rooms, parking spaces and other conveniences and services to achieve their ends.

Why cannot the church use similar principles of advertising and publicity?

WHERE ADVERTISING BEGINS

The church building itself is an advertisement of the congregation to which it belongs. Its cleanliness, the condition of its bulletin boards and signs, the sidewalks, the fences, the lights, the care of the property in general — all of these have a message of welcome or discouragement to those who enter and to those who pass by.

In a recent address to an audience of two hundred ministers, I stressed the importance of the care of church property. At the close of my remarks, the chairman asked the question: " How many of you pastors honestly feel that your churches need painting? " More than half the hands were raised.

If I were the minister of a small frame church, I think I should paint it white, and I should set it in the midst of green lawns and friendly trees and shrubs and flowers. I should keep its walls and windows clean and its steps and roof repaired. I should place it at the head of the street, or at an intersection of two main highways. I should build a tower or a steeple upon it, with perhaps a radiant cross to shine by night. And I should put my church on a hill, if possible; and these features in themselves would be good advertising and publicity.

In Chicago there is a large insurance firm whose officers have reached the conclusion that it does not matter particularly what kind of publicity material is sent out to their clients, provided that something goes out frequently to keep the name of the firm before the public. It may be a calendar or a blotter or a circular with some homely message, but the constituency is kept reminded of the firm.

If this method can be used with success in business, may it not also be applied to religion? If so, how much more effective it may become if the publicity is carefully prepared and well directed.

Paid advertising or even free publicity is practically useless unless there is a worthy church program, with definite goals to be reached; and one of the great oversights on the part of many ministers is that they do not plan their work far enough ahead or set their objectives definitely enough to direct their advertising and publicity toward these ends.

THE CHURCH PROGRAM

The first suggestion, then, is to study the church program, which might be listed under such general headings as worship, religious education, social activities, missions, properties, etc.

Certain features of a building program may be of interest to architectural and technical journals and to real-estate sections of the daily press, but may have no value whatever as religious or general news. On the other hand, the development of the religious educational program may be of practically no interest to the ordinary layman, but may be considered as of great importance to church schoolteachers and other readers of religious magazines.

For the local papers, the purchase of real estate is news; likewise the planning of a new building unit, or the installation of a church bell or a set of chimes, or the gift of a memorial organ or window.

The resignation or the appointment of a pastor is news, as is also the election of new officers or the appointment of important committees.

Social activities are always news if properly presented.

Missions and benevolent giving are news if they are " different." Comparisons, backed by statistical data, often help to create new interest in old subjects.

Special financial campaigns are news, and even routine money-raising may be news if the methods used are uncommon, or if the results achieved are beyond the ordinary. To illustrate:

A certain church owed sixteen hundred dollars for a paving assessment. The obligation was old, and no one seemed interested in it, but when the pastor divided the assessment into sixteen hundred units and sold them at a dollar each, thus clearing the debt, the episode became interesting news for that community.

The planting of a tree in the churchyard may be news if the tree is dedicated to a worthy name or purpose. There is a church in Chicago which often makes front-page news because its grounds are filled with trees that have been so dedicated with unusual services.

Newspapers are not only willing but anxious to print church news. The reason more is not published is that ministers and their publicity committees do not know how to prepare it. A single paragraph properly written is more valuable to an editor than a longer story poorly submitted.

Unlike a sermon, or the novel, short story or drama, the climax of a news story must appear at the beginning. The details follow. If copy must be cut to fit the space available in the paper, the most important items are thus preserved.

The following suggestions may be of assistance:

Never use editorial comment in news copy. One's personal opinions do not belong in news. Tell what happened, or what is planned. State the facts clearly and in simple language that everyone can understand. Use short sentences. Take out unnecessary words. Be absolutely accurate as to names, dates, places, spelling and all other details. Be impersonal and fair. Beware of controversies. Furnish clean, typewritten copy, preferably triple-spaced, with generous margins. Write your name, address and telephone number on the upper left-hand corner of the page. The editor may wish to call you for additional information.

Never include captions for your stories. These are written by the expert copyreader of the newspaper. Therefore, it is desirable that the most important item should stand out at the beginning for his attention, like the jewel on a ring.

In determining the " lead " in a news story, it is well to keep in mind six words or questions: What? When? Where? Who? Why? and How? For example:

" *What* " becomes most important when the facts speak

out for themselves, as: " three men killed," " fire burns cripple," " First Church launches building campaign."

" *When* " takes the lead if the time of the accident or event is unusual, as: " on Christmas Eve " (stranger freezes to death), " Easter morning " (crowds overflow churches), " on his mother's birthday " (son gives new hymn books).

" *Where* " assumes precedence if the place is different, as: " bank robbed on university campus," " groom deserts bride at altar," " man shoots self in League of Nations building."

" *Who* " is first, if it is: Rockefeller, Ford, the President or the king; the mayor of the city; the pastor, or another leading person in your church.

" *Why* " considers the motive, as: " girl takes poison," " bank cashier disappears," " man attempts to dynamite self."

" *How* " arouses one's curiosity, as: " plane catches fire above clouds," " two men injured in freak collision," " church janitor is electrocuted."

Which of these is outstanding in your thought? This is the " lead " of your news story. The details may follow in the order of their importance.

ADVERTISING FOR WHAT?

The main value of advertising and publicity is to develop a constituency that will support and carry out the ideals and plans of its leaders. Let us imagine, then, that our church, through its minister and his associates, has determined upon its program.

At once a flood of suggestions comes to us. If we are to plan for an expansion or the improvement of our buildings and grounds, let us consult with our leading architect and secure his recommendations for a five-year progressive development. Let us talk with the zoning commission, the artists and the landscape gardeners of our community. Here we will put in a memorial window; there the church school will plant an evergreen tree as a tribute to the memory of a former pastor; perhaps the hardware dealer will contribute the paint for decorating the church, and the men's club will see that it is applied. Such items all lend themselves to good publicity.

Are we seeking to increase our budget for the missionary program? Then let us secure stories and pictures of our foreign representative and his work. Perhaps he will send us an exhibit of costumes or curios from his field for display in the banker's or the druggist's window. We shall secure speakers from the state and perhaps the national boards; or our church school will prepare a missionary pageant and we shall furnish a news story about it to the press.

If we can get people to think and to talk of our plans, or better still, to ask questions about them, we are promoting good publicity.

From the standpoint of a theological seminary, there is probably no service more undramatic or one which has less publicity possibilities than the task of recruiting men for the Christian ministry. Many a church has taken so little interest in the question that it has not in a generation sent a single man into the pastorate from its membership. One of the prominent religious magazines refused to print our seminary's material on the subject because its editor said that seminaries were naturally expected to recruit men, and that inasmuch as the program was therefore nothing unusual, it could not receive publicity space.

We knew that unless we could get ministers and their congregations to talk about recruiting, we could not hope for any promising results from young men who might feel called to the ministry but who might be given no encouragement by those around them. Therefore, we must do something unusual.

COOPERATION THROUGH PULPIT EXCHANGES

We selected nearly one hundred of the leading ministers of the Middle West, and organized on a given day a widespread pulpit exchange in the interests of recruiting, reaching from Denver to Detroit and from Duluth to St. Louis. The messages of these ministers were gathered and printed in advance and fifty thousand copies were distributed in the area to be covered.

What was the result? Multitudes were reached with the old message in a new way. Young men inclined toward the ministry, who hesitated to talk with friends, felt free to counsel with strangers about the choice of a life work. Newspapers and religious magazines became interested, and a foundation was laid for follow-up correspondence and personal interviews, with the result that the following summer our enrollment was greatly increased.

The movement cost one thousand dollars, but a friend who heard one of the messages became interested and paid the bill with a personal check. Later, other larger financial contributions were received which were traced directly to this pulpit exchange. After long experience, it is our opinion that whenever a church promotes a forward movement intelligently, and with proper publicity, almost without exception interested friends will be found who will gladly pay the bills.

We have often wondered why this kind of advertising

could not be applied to the church. Suppose some civic enterprise of universal interest is to be promoted in a county, city or town. Why not arrange for an exchange of ministers? Or perhaps it is Youth Movement day or Boy Scout day — why not turn over the church service to the young people? Or it may be that the church school is to have a special celebration — why not have an exchange of departmental officers and teachers to emphasize the occasion? Such program changes are news because they are " different."

OTHER FORMS OF ADVERTISING

Not all advertising or publicity is confined to print. John Wanamaker's great department store in Philadelphia attracts customers by its organ concerts; Marshall Field's in Chicago is famous for its window displays; the Methodist Temple in the Chicago Loop attracts attention by its steeple; and the Straus Building by its Westminster chimes.

One of the best advertising features of the Chicago Theological Seminary is its tower, rising majestically to a height of 172 feet above the ground. Its turrets are lit by night, and it is seen daily by thousands of people passing on the Midway. Lorado Taft called it " the flower on the plant." Without this tower, the seminary buildings would scarcely be noticed by passing multitudes.

Many churches possess windows of rare design and color, but only a few illuminate them from the inside so that their glory may be seen at night. What an inspiration it would be, for example, on Christmas Eve, to see such windows alight and presenting to friend and stranger alike the message of the Good Shepherd, or the birth of the Christ child!

Many mediums of advertising and publicity are available to the church, such as:

The religious and secular press.

Weekly bulletins and monthly or quarterly publications.

Annual calendars and year books, directories, reports, etc.

Display cards for hotels, depots, street cars, buses, and other public places.

Pocket cards and admission tickets.

Pulpit and other public announcements.

The radio and the telephone.

Attractive buildings and grounds.

Flags, banners and special decorations.

Electric and painted signs.

Bulletin boards and billboards.

Bells and chimes.

Special mimeographed or printed leaflets and booklets.

Paperweights and other souvenirs.

Stereopticon and motion pictures.

Church stationery.

Personal correspondence and form letters.

Concerts, pageants and athletic programs.

Denominational literature emphasizing the larger activities of the church.

THE MINISTER AND THE PRESS

Ministers are likely to be too modest and to shrink from publicity. This attitude is a mistake. They are public leaders, appointed to influence the thought of the community. Content to address hundreds from their pulpits, they are overlooking the opportunity to reach thousands through the press. We knew a distinguished preacher of national reputa-

tion who, preceding his appointments, refused to furnish copy to the newspapers of any city. He said that he would " go around the block " before he would look at his picture in the paper. He was humble, earnest and conscientious. We asked him if he were not thinking of himself rather than of his cause. He saw his error and revised his policy. From that time forward, he sent advance outlines of his addresses, together with photographs or cuts, to the publicity committee or to the leading papers of each city he was to visit. His stories were widely published and his influence was multiplied many fold. Later he was elected the national moderator of his denomination.

At a crucial time in his political career, the governor of a Middle Western state was scheduled to give his closing campaign address at an outdoor picnic where great crowds were expected to gather. When the day arrived, it was cold and a steady rain was falling. Only a few friends were present, and there was very little enthusiasm. The picnic was a failure, but the governor's campaign was a success. Why? Because the governor's address had been prepared and distributed to the press in advance, and it was read by thousands in their homes.

We should be careful that we do not promote a " forced publicity," reaching beyond the merits of our work. It is better to have a good program and " satisfied customers " without publicity, than to have all the promotional publicity in the world, with discontent in the church.

If, then, our goal is worthy, our program definite and our organization complete, let us have the courage and let us develop the skill to tell our story not only to those who may be present on Sunday mornings to hear our preaching, but

to the outside world as well, through the many channels of advertising and publicity which lie open on every hand.

(Note: For those who wish to use cuts and half-tones to make their printed matter more attractive, reference is suggested to the Cobb Shinn Co., 40 Jackson Place, Indianapolis, Indiana. This firm issues catalogues entitled " Type Warmers," which offer inexpensive electrotypes for almost every purpose, especially those of national interest such as illustrations for holidays, patriotic occasions, etc.)

Chapter Six

CHURCH FINANCE

PROBABLY no subject is of greater concern to ministers, or of larger significance to successful administration, than that of church finance.

Most of us seem hard pressed to meet our bills, and it is almost out of the question to promote new enterprises. Yet there is not less money in the world today than there has been in the past. We have had no earthquakes, famines, pestilences or other national calamities. Our banks are filled with money seeking profitable investment.

It is true that wealth is changing hands. My neighbor's house has been taken over by his mortgage holder. The apartment building on which some of us had bonds has been reorganized, and the investments represented by our stock certificates have fluctuated in value from time to time, but the country's wealth is still intact.

And if, in my church work, I am ever inclined to be discouraged by the condition of worldly affairs, I still remember the words of a song I once heard at a revival meeting — " My Father is rich in houses and lands " — and I think too of the psalmist's statement that " the cattle upon a thousand hills " are still His. Yes, upon a hundred thousand hills.

When we compare our living standards with those of many foreign countries, we know for a certainty that America is

rich. Granted, then, that there is sufficient money in a given
community, how shall we attract the proper share of it to the
work of the church?

MANAGEMENT ATTRACTS CAPITAL

Money, or the lack of it, is not a problem in itself. The
problem to be faced is one of management, for good management attracts capital as well to the church as to channels of
business.

The first step in church finance is to set up a worthy program of service — one in which all the people will have confidence and in which they will cooperate.

Then a budget should be outlined, showing the estimated
receipts and expenses for the year and the amount of money
that must be raised to carry out the program. The treasurer's
financial statement for the previous year, including a complete list of assets and liabilities, will have an important
bearing on the new budget.

In the preparation of the budget, all organizations represented should be consulted, and likewise all paid employees,
from the minister to the janitor. Many valuable suggestions
come from sources whence they are least expected.

The pastor's salary should not be minimized. It is the
most important item in the budget. As a rule, the salaries of
the employed staff of a church will be just about equal to the
costs of operation, maintenance and promotion.

The item of benevolences in a church budget is not op-
tional. It is required as a vital element in the Christian program. It is significant that those churches which have carried out faithfully and to the best of their ability the spirit
of the " Great Commission " have themselves prospered.

The larger the vision, the more generous seems to be the support.

Where previous deficits must be included in a new budget, it is best to cover them by routine receipts, such as the open offerings, so that all new pledges may be applied to new work. It is unwise to count upon last year's unpaid pledges as assets, because at the end of the current year about the same number of accounts will be outstanding.

When the new budget has been recommended by the trustees or the official board and adopted by the congregation of the church (this is done usually at the annual meeting), it is then time to organize and promote the every-member-canvass.

CONDUCTING A CANVASS

It is well to send two or three informational and inspirational letters to the prospective givers in advance of the canvass, from four days to a week apart, also to have the minister deliver at least one sermon on stewardship or on the missionary work of the denomination, and likewise to ask one or more laymen to address the congregation briefly on the financial condition of the church and the objects of the campaign.

The solicitors should go in pairs, and enough workers should be enrolled so that each team may be assigned not more than from three to five names for calls, and thus be enabled to complete the canvass in a single day. The subsequent week may be used for a follow-up of those who were away or could not be seen on the day of the campaign. Rarely should the canvass for a current budget, including the follow-up, cover a period of more than a week.

In larger financial campaigns for special objects, such as

new buildings or new equipment, a longer period of preparation is necessary, usually from one to three months according to the amount of money to be raised, the constituency to be covered and the difficulties to be overcome. The time for actual solicitation may range from a week to a month, with from one to three months for follow-up.

FIVE PHASES OF CAMPAIGNS

There are five distinct phases in such campaigns:

(1) *Survey*. The preliminary survey should review the historic background, analyze problems and statistics, study budgets of this and similar institutions, compile lists of names of both workers and prospective givers, and carefully tabulate all information to be used later in the campaign.

(2) *Advertising and publicity*. When the program is determined, it should be made familiar to the public. This may be done through:

(a) Sermons, radio and other public addresses.

(b) Conferences and special meetings with leaders.

(c) Stories in newspapers and magazines.

(d) Correspondence and form letters.

(e) Leaflets, booklets, announcements in bulletins, etc.

The value of such advance advertising and publicity is threefold: (a) It increases the faith and courage of those already in sympathy with the movement; (b) it overcomes possible opposition in advance of the campaign; (c) it creates new friends, both workers and prospective financial contributors, for the campaign to be launched.

(3) *Organization of the working forces*. Just as an army must have a general, so a campaign organization must have the right chairman. Plenty of time should be taken to select

and to interest the key man. Without him a successful financial campaign can hardly be conducted. The minister
should never serve as chairman.

Then in their turn come the division leaders, captains and
individual solicitors. It is well to have a special gifts committee quietly at work to obtain all possible larger gifts before the general campaign is launched. If properly organized
and directed, this committee will raise from a third to a half
of the amount needed, and such an achievement will be a
great stimulus to the seekers of smaller gifts. As a rule, about
75 per cent of the money to be secured will come from approximately 25 per cent of the contributors.

(4) *The actual canvass or period of solicitation.* In military terms, no matter how strong the forces there must be a
battle before there can be a victory. So it is with a financial
campaign. There must be a definite time set aside for the
solicitation of prospective givers. The constituency must be
enlarged.

Names should be distributed to the workers and charged
out to them for follow-up. Regular report meetings should
be held (daily, if possible). Slogans should be created, goals
set, and instruction and encouragement given freely. The
campaign is now launched and must proceed aggressively.

As a barrage protects an advancing army in battle, so continued advertising and publicity encourage both the workers
and the prospective contributors in a financial campaign.

No person should be allowed to solicit subscriptions who
has not himself made a pledge.

(5) *The follow-up.* Because so many emergencies arise
and so many people are sick or absent or for other reason cannot be seen during the period of intensive solicitation, there
must be a comprehensive and thorough follow-up if the cam-

paign is to attain the highest possible success. Generally, from 25 per cent to 50 per cent of the funds needed will come from the follow-up if it is properly organized and directed.

Expect every helper to complete his task. Tell him so by newspaper, circular letter, telephone and personal interview. Keep him enthusiastic until the work is finished. No campaign is over until every prospect has been asked to give. When the goal has been reached, have a celebration or a recognition banquet, and publicly express praise and appreciation to all who have had part in the movement.

It was my privilege to serve in an eighty thousand dollar campaign for a new parish house. Because the membership of the parish in question was largely transient, it was considered best to raise the complete amount before beginning construction. When the building was finished, the church provided a " Victory Banquet " to which were invited not only those who had taken part in the campaign, but every laborer who had worked on the building — excavators, bricklayers, plasterers, carpenters, plumbers, steam fitters, electricians, decorators and all the rest — and together they celebrated the " completion of the temple." It was an unusual fellowship, and for that reason it attracted the attention of the newspapers, and the church went forward enthusiastically to new achievements.

OTHER FORMS OF COOPERATION

One reason why the subject of financial support is so objectionable in the average church is that it is often the only opportunity for cooperation offered to the members. It is almost comparable to the old problem of " taxation without representation." Take, for example, the new member who is received into the church. About the first if not the only approach that is made to him is in behalf of the budget. He is asked to share in the payment of an expense for which he does not feel directly responsible. What, then, is his reaction? Either he resents the financial appeal, or he makes a small subscription in a routine way and believes that his obligation has been met.

Put the same member to work on an intelligent survey of the community, or on a well organized budget committee, or on one of the many other attractive departments of the church program, and he will at once take a new interest in the finances of the church and often will not only contribute more liberally himself, but will uncover resources previously unknown.

From my own experience I recall the case of an institution which solicited me regularly and to which I contributed two dollars a year. Unexpectedly I was made the denominational representative on this organization's finance committee. With a new interest in the organization, I raised my gift to ten dollars. Then I was appointed chairman of the finance committee, and my pledge went to twenty-five dollars. Within a year I was elected also chairman of a special campaign committee, and in spite of the fact that my income had shrunk somewhat, I increased my subscription to fifty dollars. The cause was the same, but with the added responsibility my enthusiasm grew proportionately, expressing itself quite naturally in greater contributions. Ministers should be aware of the value of this psychological phenomenon in promoting the program of the church.

In a financial campaign, the workers should be recruited, if possible, from the organization directly involved, but it is not necessary or desirable to confine the constituency to this list. Parents of the children in the church school, for instance, whether church members or not, are legitimate prospects for financial support; likewise philanthropic and public-spirited citizens, and especially those whose business is benefited directly by a stabilized community through the development of personal character. In one instance, 10 per cent of the cost of a new suburban church was subscribed by real-estate dealers outside the membership of the church because the dealers felt that the community in general, and their own business in particular, would be helped by the building of this church.

It requires the expenditure of real nervous energy to solicit pledges from one's friends and neighbors, just as it does for salesmen to secure orders for merchandise, but there is no satisfaction quite equal to that of having helped in a successful financial campaign for the church. There is something constructive about it. Many a worker who has shrunk from going out to solicit funds for the first time has afterward looked forward eagerly to the next opportunity.

OPPORTUNITIES FOR GIVING

One of the most sacred and satisfactory ways to secure funds for property improvements or for additions to plant or equipment is through memorial gifts. People like to provide special objects in memory of loved ones who have died. For this reason, they give pulpit Bibles, chancel furniture, bells and chimes, organs, hymnbooks, art glass windows, new buildings, and many other items for the beautification and enlargement of the church. Where else could their devotion be more appropriately expressed?

The reason that more such gifts are not made is that we

do not offer the definite opportunities. If the minister and his board would take time to study the situation, to consult with artists, architects and other experts, and to issue a memorial booklet which would name and describe attractively and somewhat in detail the improvements that were needed together with their approximate cost, so that their merits could be considered intelligently by those who might become interested, they would be surprised to see how quickly the desired goals would be reached.

I cannot speak too highly of the distinguished service which has been rendered to churches by professional campaign organizations, some of which are conducted by consecrated Christian men of great ability whose counsel has prevented many a costly mistake and whose wide experience has made it possible to discover a short cut to the results desired. Some of them operate on a commission basis; others, for a fee. The cost of such professional service is usually estimated as approximately one year's interest on the amount to be raised. For safe estimates in budget-building, five per cent should be added for promotion and collection, and another five per cent for shrinkage.

Financial campaigns should not be thought of lightly. It should be remembered that money is the symbol or the equivalent of consecrated work or service. If a man earns five dollars a day and gives fifty dollars to the church, he is in reality giving ten days of his life.

THE MINISTER'S SHARE

Ministers, as a rule, pledge too much of their personal incomes to the budgets of the church. They are so interested in the work that they subscribe out of proportion to the gifts of others with similar resources. It is my feeling that an organization is not strong which must draw its support from the paid members of its staff. I do not think a pastor should pledge more than he would if he were not the minister of the church.

The budget of a church is important. However, it should not be our master but our servant, our guide. It may be altered as conditions change.

The financial records of the treasurer should be kept so clearly and so simply that a comparison of actual receipts and expenses may be made with the budget every month or more often if desired.

Shall we " balance the budget "? For business, yes; for churches, not necessarily. Most churches running on a balanced budget would be dead spiritually. Material things would come first. A certain proportion of " faith " is justified. In the average church, not more than 50 per cent of the members make any regular pledges. Why not work a little more intensively on the other 50 per cent, and go forward with the promotion of a growing program?

Never permit the use of benevolence money for the payment of current bills. It is better to have two treasurers, each with a separate bank account, than to yield to this temptation. Some churches pay their treasurers a nominal salary, and it is a good investment, for they have a right then to expect attendance and reports at meetings of the board, and there is less embarrassment in asking for the provisions of bonds and audits.

Do you have " pillars of the church " in your congregation? It is better not to depend upon them too much for generous pledges to the current budget or for substantial checks to meet a deficit. The risk is too great. They may move some day or die, and then it is difficult to close the

ranks. These men and women are worthy of more challeng-
ing tasks. They should be improving the church properties through special gifts, and their loyalty and generosity
should be made available for the larger work of the denomination in its world-wide field.

It is a justified recognition to publish the names of subscribers to a budget, but the amounts of the gifts should not
be included. Delinquent accounts should not be advertised.

Pledges should be acknowledged by the treasurer or other
proper official in order that misunderstanding in the collection of accounts may be avoided.

If a letter of information concerning the finances of the
church were sent with each quarterly or monthly statement
to delinquent subscribers, the average collections received
would be doubled.

RAISING MONEY

There are many ways to raise money for the church. Here
are several.

(1) *The every-member-canvass.*
>   (a) By direct solicitation, with personal follow-up.
>   (b) By public presentation to the congregation,
>   with follow-up as needed.
>   (c) By mail.
>   (d) By telephone (recommended only in apart-
>   ment house and hotel communities).

(2) *The annual roll call at the Sunday morning service.*

(3) *The " Joash Chest "* (see II Chron. 24:1–14). This
has many variations. It may include a chest or a thank-offer-
ing box at the front of the church auditorium or at the
entrance door.

(4) *Assumption of renewals of previous pledges.* This may be done only unless or until otherwise notified. Solicitation of new members, and in special cases where personal approach seems justified.

(5) *Miscellaneous special projects.*

It is our judgment that by far the best method is the every-member-canvass, with direct solicitation and personal follow-up, though there is wisdom in varying this plan occasionally so that the people may not tire of it.

Some churches have awakened new interest in the homes by conducting a junior canvass a week ahead of the regular campaign. It is set up exactly like the senior canvass, and provides for a solicitation of the young people by their own leaders. The gain is not so much the additional pledges received as the education and training of the juniors, and, incidentally, a new approach to the parents who, by the time the senior canvass is launched, have become rather familiar with the needs of the new year's budget.

Well conducted campaigns are a tonic for a church. Choirs, orchestras, bands and drama groups cannot be held together without public performances. Preparation leads naturally to action. There are successful churches which never finish one campaign without beginning another. These churches are growing because they have life within them.

The values of a campaign are more than financial. The institution and its program have been made known to the public. New friends have been added; new workers have been found and trained; good fellowship and a broader understanding have been created both for the local church and for the larger interests of the Christian cause.

Chapter Seven

CHRISTIAN STEWARDSHIP

AS A LAYMAN I am often asked for my opinion on the subject of Christian stewardship. Not long ago I wrote an article for the *New Century Leader,* on " How to Get Rich by Giving Everything Away." In this message I took the stand that all great men give away more than they receive from others. How else could they be great?

There are many lessons for us in the Bible concerning stewards and stewardship, as in Luke 12:42–44, Luke 16:1–8, and I Cor. 4:1–2, for instance.

According to the dictionary, a steward is " a person entrusted with the management of estates or affairs not his own."

Perhaps most of us have thought of stewardship as pertaining to money or financial affairs. I like to think of it as covering life itself. The general conception of Christian stewardship is to put God first, as the owner of all; treat your whole income as a sacred trust; give generously.

My conception of stewardship is not only to give generously, but to use generously. I may not wish to dispose of my automobile, but I am none the poorer for giving a person a ride. All of us have not only material resources, but we have talents, influence and powers of many kinds that grow by use and which are given us as a trust from God.

" Are you cold? " asked a strange woman of a little girl as

she knelt to put her arm around the shivering little form on a winter night.

" I was until you kissed me," came the tearful reply.

This is what I mean by " stewardship."

The abundant life is not a struggle for existence resulting in the survival of the fittest. Our real satisfactions come from unselfish service. According to Rousseau, " every man goes down to the grave carrying in his clutched hands only that which he has given away."

The man who believes that the world owes him a living and goes out to take whatever he can get from his fellow men is doomed to inner failure; while the man who feels that he has been born into a world of opportunity for service is destined for success.

SOME GREAT EXAMPLES

One of the most prominent laymen ever engaged in religious work in North America was Marion Lawrance, for many years the general secretary of the International Sunday School Association. I knew him intimately and traveled with him extensively. With thousands of people ready to pay him tribute on every hand, and anxious to do his will, he never took anything for himself, but sought always to honor his associates and to magnify their points of excellence. As a result, it was said of him that the brilliance of those who were uplifted by the power of his noble life cast its reflected light back upon him and made him great.

All outstanding men whom we recognize as public servants are great because they give freely, not only of their material resources, but of their personalities, their minds, their talents. Peter had this thought when he said to the lame man, " Silver and gold have I none; but such as I have give I thee." And he gave him health, which was a far better gift than wealth.

Jesus was familiar with this principle when he told the parable of the Talents. Before taking a long and possibly dangerous journey into a foreign country, a man divided his wealth among his three trusted servants, giving five talents to one, two to another and one to the third, according to their recognized ability. The first and second servants doubled their investments while he was gone, but, in a spirit of timidity and fear, the third servant buried his talent without even trying to use it. Because of this, his master took away what little he had and gave it to the one who had shown the greatest initiative.

It is always better to wear out than to rust out. Good machinery, however, neither wears out nor rusts out if kept clean and thoroughly lubricated. Neither do men wear out or rust out by constructive thought and active service, but rather by fear and disinclination to use the talents bestowed upon them.

The examples of Toyohiko Kagawa of Japan and Mahatma Gandhi of India are living testimonies of how men may become rich by giving away their worldly possessions. They are truly carrying out the admonition of Jesus: " He that is least among you all, the same shall be great."

A BUSINESSMAN ON STEWARDSHIP

Quite recently I sought out a prominent businessman, a leader in his church and in many civic enterprises, a man of maturity and of successful business experience. I wanted his counsel on stewardship. This was his story: " When entering business nearly fifty years ago, I decided to be a tither, but this did not satisfy me. I made a contract with myself and the Lord that no matter how much or little I earned, I would give a tenth, but that if and as I exceeded a certain minimum amount of income which I thought I needed, I would grade my giving, according to the income received, up to 20 per cent. From that time on, I have prospered. I always have money for worthy causes, and not only has this plan of a double tithe been a source of general satisfaction to me, but I have felt the sacredness of my trust so deeply that I really would not dare to do less than I promised. If anything, I am likely to do more."

Money-making is a " game " that many businessmen find attractive. Some become so engrossed in it that they neglect their families and barter the lives of their fellow men for the god they call " success." But such a course does not bring satisfaction. One of the chief reasons that led to my decision to give my life to the business side of religious work was the observation that men of power and influence turn away from their financial and business enterprises to seek the compensations that come from the construction and maintenance of churches, schools and other character-building and philanthropic enterprises. After wide observation, I have reached the conclusion that all of the world's wealth may be as nothing, for it will not buy the smile of a child, the song of a bird, the loyalty of a friend, or restore a loved one from sickness to health.

It is the use we make of our material resources, and of our time and talents — the stewardship of God's gifts to us — that counts in the destiny of mankind, and that brings us the enjoyment of peaceful sleep and the inspiration to live. Our resources are unlimited, but they do not take on reality or bring happiness to us until we pass them on to others. " Give me only the tools with which to work; my service belongs to you," is a good slogan for a Christian steward.

The recent years of world-wide depression have taught us many lessons. We have seen financial kingdoms fall. The fires of genius have been quenched and the spirit of men has been broken. Business success has turned to failure, and people have asked, " Where can security be found? " If ever in the world's history opportunity knocked at our door, it is now. Today is the time for character to reveal itself, to put fear to flight and to restore confidence. Above all things, let us, as Christians, remain steadfast to our trust. Let us not be limited by circumstances, but let us create new environments that good will may come to men and the spirit of peace and brotherhood be established throughout the earth.

STEWARDSHIP AND SACRIFICE

I do not know of any institution which does as much as the church to plant in a child's life the ideals of Christian character.

In Mark 8:34–36, we read from the words of Jesus:

" Whosoever will come after me, let him deny himself, and take up his cross, and follow me.

" For whosoever will save his soul shall lose it; but whosoever shall lose his life for my sake, . . . the same shall save it.

" For what shall it profit a man, if he shall gain the whole world, and lose his own soul? "

We can make our church a watchtower and a lighthouse for a dark and needy world.

To carry out our program fully, as it should be carried out, may require sacrifice, and sacrifice means giving. " You can *give* without *loving,* but you can't *love* without *giving.*"

John 3:16 tells us that " God *so* loved the world that he gave his only begotten Son " for us!

The question, then, that we must ask ourselves is this: " As Christian stewards, what will *we* do, for Him? "

CHAPTER EIGHT

THE SEXTON

THE CHURCH janitor is an important figure. He can make or mar almost any program promoted by the minister. He can cause the mechanics of the church to run as smoothly and as noiselessly as oiled machinery, or he can throw it into devastating confusion.

"A good janitor," says one clergyman, "is a gift of God, but for some wise reason that gift is very infrequently bestowed. Most janitors have no conception of the difference between cold air and fresh air. Janitors can undo any minister's public work by failing to ventilate or heat the church properly and by neglecting to keep it neat and clean. I had a church at which I preached in the morning to a shivering congregation; immediately following there was a Sunday school service which was almost impossible to conduct because by this time the rooms were filled with smoke; at night the temperature was above 85 degrees. Some janitors I have known seem systematically to choose the time of prayer for shaking down the furnace, and they rattle it until the prayer is concluded. One morning I prayed for fifteen minutes to see if I could not get beyond this noise, and barely made it. I think the janitor must have quit from exhaustion."

Of course, there is the sexton's side also. "Church members seem to think I ought to be a mind reader," says a faithful janitor. "They want everything in readiness for their meetings without giving me the slightest information as to the program, or advice as to my duties. I am criticized constantly, though I try to do my best. Sometimes I wonder if my pastor is a Christian. I wish that seminaries would require of every theological student at least a year's training as the janitor of a church before they graduate him into the ministry."

The large city church really has no janitor problem comparable to that of smaller churches, for it generally secures an expert from outside the congregation or a staff sufficient for the demands of the work, and both hires and fires without embarrassment according to the satisfaction of the service rendered. Some institutions employ engineers to supervise their plant equipment at salaries as high as four thousand dollars annually.

The smaller churches likewise have no serious difficulties, for the very nature of their problems often points the way to their solution. Much of the service needed is rendered on a volunteer basis, perhaps by the minister himself or a member of his family, or by one of the trustees, the women's organization, or by some interested member of the congregation.

THE DIFFICULTIES OF SUBSTITUTES

The real trouble is found in the medium-sized church which can afford neither an expert nor the services of a full-time man. As one minister of eighteen years' experience testifies:

" Either we must employ a man who gives us part time or we must take the services of a derelict who has retired from the farm, or broken down under some form of manual labor, having had no experience as an indoor man until long after his habits are set, and with no real appreciation of the spirit of the work of the church. As to the temperature for our meetings, if he is comfortable in a coat as he moves about, why should any of the congregation complain of the cold?"

Many churches employ high school students as caretakers, but rarely with satisfaction. They require too much supervision and seldom take an interest in their work.

Several ministers have told me of their experiences with high school boys as janitors.

"One of the boys we hired used the basement for a 'hookey room' to which he brought other truants for 'smokers,' to the embarrassment of the church."

"They are imbued with the spirit of the gang, and usually bring a crowd of boys with them. They are rough in the building, carelessly leave the lights turned on, and seem to care little for the property of the church."

"We use high school boys employed and supervised by the women's society. While the grounds have been kept in good condition, there are many requirements inside the church which the boys do not understand. Especially are they unable to make necessary repairs, and therefore the buildings and equipment are not kept in order as they might be were an older person in charge."

SUPERVISING THE SEXTON

Who should supervise the sexton's work? Some feel that this is the responsibility of the chairman of the board of trustees; others, of the house or buildings and grounds committee, or the women's association. Perhaps an equal number think that the activities of the caretaker are so closely allied to those of the minister that the janitor should serve under the pastor's direction. There is merit in this suggestion, inasmuch as the sexton is a member of the paid staff and the minister would naturally be at the head of those employed.

" The pastor is the man most intimately connected with the running of the church," declares a clergyman who has been successful in his parish. " Whether he likes it or not, much responsibility for the ordering and arranging of the church building is entirely his, particularly all that relates to the immediate conduct of the church program. Any conflict of authority is an infringement of the minister's efficiency. The fault lies not with the janitor in such cases, but with the board or women's society that presumes to interfere. The minister can be gracious, but he had better have it clearly understood from the beginning that he is in charge."

" I think the minister instead of the church board ought to hire and fire the janitor," says another pastor, " and in that way he could keep him more under his control."

" No valid request from the minister should be either ignored or obstructed," says the leader of a prosperous church. " In any case where cooperation cannot be secured happily, the minister should insist upon a new employee, who will be nominated by him to the buildings and grounds committee before the final arrangement is ratified by the board."

" The women's society knows so much more than the men about housecleaning and the general arrangement of church equipment that it seems only reasonable in our church that the women should be in charge."

And yet: " Our janitor rebelled this year because he had too many bosses. He was hired by the trustees but directed by the women. They sent him constantly on errands, with packages of clothing for the poor, to return Mrs. Brown's silverware after the church supper, etc., until he felt there was no end to his work."

" I do the best I can," says one janitor, " and yet they scold me because my broom or vacuum cleaner hasn't reached all the dust in the corners, or my dust mop has failed to find a cobweb, or perhaps a gown has been soiled on a church pew that I thought was clean."

It should be taken for granted that if the sexton is directed by the house committee, the women's society should be represented on the committee.

As to a title, not all churches use the term " janitor " or " sexton." Some dignify the position by such names as " custodian," " caretaker," " engineer " or " superintendent of buildings and grounds." Such nomenclatures are of considerable help in matters of committee representation or public recognition, especially when the sexton is a member of the church.

Should the janitor be employed from the membership of the church?

" Yes," say many ministers, especially of the smaller organizations. " Most of the churches demand more work than would be justified by the salaries paid. This extra service can come only through the loyalty and love of the janitor for his church."

And on the other hand: " The house committee was composed of three members, two of whom were in the same family. They engaged as janitor their grandfather and father-in-law. The man was too old for the job. His work was a failure, and yet because he was a member of the church no one had the courage either to speak to him personally or to suggest his dismissal."

" We had to discharge our janitor, a member of the church, because of general inefficiency. As a result, his whole family left the church, and the situation was very embarrassing."

" Our janitor is one of our church deacons, densely ignorant, with no appreciation of ventilation, cleanliness or the other needs of the general situation. Don't ask me why we keep him. We would know what to do if he were not a member of the church."

" We had an old couple, faithful members of our church, but they became very gossipy and brought trouble to several of the organizations of the church. What could we do? "

WRITTEN CONTRACTS

Some ministers feel that all their janitor troubles would be ended if written contracts could be made at the time of employment, specifying the exact duties to be covered. Our judgment is that just the reverse would be true, for every growing church program is subject to constant change. No contract in the world can command the individual interest and initiative which are so necessary to the work of the Christian church.

Of course, there is probably no minister these days who would attempt to imitate the Roman centurion and be so bold as to say to his janitor, " Do this! " or " Do that! " As one pastor of mature experience puts it, he suggests to his custodian: " There has been a lot of dirt tracked into the east entrance. I suspect that it had better be cleaned up before Wednesday evening." " The kitchen floor has been in bad shape since the last dinner. Perhaps it should be scrubbed before the grease begins to smell too badly." Or, " It might appear better, when people come in, if you would put your broom and dust cloths out of sight whenever you are not using them, rather than to leave them on the altar or the communion table." There is no doubt that tactfulness on the minister's part would go a long way toward resolving many of the complications of personal relationships.

The problems of janitor employment, supervision and service are really not as serious as has been intimated. The trouble lies with the organization. If we do not hire the right man, or pay him sufficient wages, or furnish him with proper tools, or center authority in one place, or make his duties clear, or train him for his tasks, or give him recognition for work well done, the difficulty is not with the sexton, but with the management of the church. We ought to provide him with a workshop and good tools, a dressing room with lavatory, a storeroom, and such other equipment as will help to make him efficient and dignify his position.

There are many spiritual-minded, faithful and well trained men and women in the janitor service of the church. The work of ministers would be seriously handicapped without them. Only recently we heard of an Iowa janitor who remained loyally with his church for fifty years, to the satisfaction of all concerned.

" Our sexton has missed only two services in thirteen years," testifies one minister. " His salary means nothing as the measure of his service. He does what needs to be done because he loves the church. He rings the bell on time to the second, actually holding a watch in one hand while he grasps the rope in the other."

Another janitor said to his pastor: " I cannot preach the gospel, I cannot help the sick or comfort the sorrowing, but I can do the work of Christ by keeping the church clean and beautiful, and in that way, I can help to lighten your tasks as our minister." Such men are worth their weight in gold.

There are two important rules to keep in mind with regard to the janitor problem, the solution of which is within the reach of any church:

(1) Have the courage and take the pains necessary to employ the right person for the work — the best available, either from within or without the congregation of the church.

(2) Having found the right person, clearly state his duties, take time to train him for the needs of his work. Make him an expert. Kindle the spark of cooperative enthusiasm within his heart by establishing a true partnership with him. Share his problems. Commend his good deeds. Honor him privately and publicly, and rejoice always in his success.

The following list of duties is furnished as suggestive of what might be expected of the church janitor. It is by no means complete, because every local situation will determine its own needs.

DUTIES OF SEXTONS

(1) *Buildings.* Air the church buildings before public sessions, and keep them ventilated during meetings if the weather permits. Windows and doors should not be opened or closed during services, except as requested by the minister or the officers of the church. Avoid moving about.

Pick up papers, and dust all furniture and equipment.

Vacuum, sweep, mop or wax floors, as needed.

Provide and arrange furniture for all regular and special meetings. Put in order when programs are finished.

If there is a church bell, ring it regularly, at times agreed.

Operate heating plants to achieve economy and efficiency, but in such a way as not to interfere with any of the church services. Boilers, valves, traps, pipes, etc., should be inspected, cleaned, adjusted and repaired once a year, or more often if required. Keep temperature at 68 to 70 degrees in winter season, and make rooms as cool as possible in summer.

See to burning or proper disposition of all refuse, garbage, etc., to keep properties attractive and safe from fire risks. Dispose of ashes at regular intervals; use metal containers rather than wood.

Become familiar with the entire plant and its equipment.

Minor repairs: Keep a set of good tools. Replace broken window glass. Do small jobs of carpentering. Fix locks, hinges, catches, hooks, chairs and pews; tighten everything that is loose, such as shelves, pew-racks, etc. Have paint-brush, varnish can and gluepot handy. Much money can be saved the church in this way, and a great deal of satisfaction will come not only to the caretaker but to the congregation. Such items as cannot be covered should be reported promptly in writing to the chairman of the house committee or other proper officials. Carry a notebook and pencil at all times for recording items of this kind and for those that may need your later attention.

Appear neat and well dressed at public services. Listen much, talk little. Keep on friendly terms with everybody. Stay out of sight as much as possible. Your work is to be a stage manager rather than an actor. The church belongs to the congregation; the sexton is employed to take care of it. Avoid a commanding attitude. Don't try to be a " policeman " on the premises.

Oil everything that squeaks — machinery, hinges, chair casters, etc.

Keep all brooms, brushes, dust cloths, tools and surplus equipment put away.

Unlock and open doors as required for all meetings. At close of sessions see that lights are out, water turned off, fires banked and under control, and doors and windows locked.

Allow no dead lamps or broken fixtures. Keep the lights shining brightly for the church.

Wash windows, glass doors to bookcases, etc.

Keep lavatories and toilets clean; furnish towels, soap and other supplies, as needed.

Provide vases and water for chancel flowers.

Put hymnbooks right side up (with front cover forward) and in order in pew-racks. Post hymn numbers on bulletin boards for Sunday services. See that weekly calendars are furnished to the ushers.

Keep clocks wound and regulated.

(2) *Grounds.* Seed, water, weed and cut lawns, as needed. Trim trees and shrubbery, care for flower beds, rake leaves and keep everything in good condition.

Clear yards of papers and rubbish daily.

Keep sidewalks, steps and entrances swept in summer and clear of snow and ice in winter.

Set up copy for bulletin boards, as directed.

Raise and lower the flag on special days.

Note: Under certain conditions, the parsonage may be included with the care of other church properties.

Make your work a sacred vocation — not just a means of livelihood. Appreciate the purpose of the church, and try to help the pastor in the spirit of his high calling.

CHAPTER NINE

THE USE OF TIME

THE MINISTER is a busy man. I wonder sometimes if he is not too busy? Too busy to answer his mail; too busy to make pastoral calls; too busy to listen sympathetically to those who come to him with their troubles; too busy to set up an efficient organizational staff; too busy to be pleasant, even to his family.

Why is he so busy? Is it because he has overemphasized the details which have pressed upon him for attention until he has lost sight of the main objective, the larger program? Sometimes he finds himself on a bypath, and may not know how to return to the right road. He keeps getting more fussy. He works longer hours and begins to crave sympathy from those about him. He complains about the high pressure under which he is working. Even his best friends begin to let him alone, and life becomes a burden.

If only, at such times, he could take a trip in an aeroplane, or stand at the top of a high mountain, so that he could look down and see that his whole field of labor is less than a speck in the universe, it would help him to get the right perspective. He needs to work less and think more. His problem is to find quicker ways to cover his tasks.

DETAILS THAT HELP OR HINDER

Perhaps he is writing too many letters or making them too long. Is he entertaining visitors for an hour, when ten minutes would be sufficient? Maybe he is spending too much time in the preparation of his sermons, when he ought to be out among his friends, at play. Perhaps he needs an office or a typewriter or an automobile. Somewhere, there is an answer to his problem.

Frequently a minister is interrupted by callers who are strangers, some of them seeking information, financial aid or endorsements, others coming with something to sell. With solicitors he often wastes hours in the office or study, and interviews are ended many times by nothing less than nervous fatigue on the part of either the minister or the salesman. Generally the minister yields, but not from conviction. His surrender in such cases is rather due to a certain lack of moral courage. He should listen to each appeal with an open mind, then make his decision quickly, and abide by it. There is always a time in an interview when it is just as easy to close the discussion as to continue it. The minister may, without offense, rise and thank the caller for his visit. Or he may ask to be excused to keep another engagement, being careful to do so in a courteous manner, for the influence of the stranger may help or hinder him in ways that he cannot always foresee.

A busy minister once briefly received a salesman from a publishing house. Feeling that the books were good for the purpose for which they were intended, he gave the caller a written endorsement and sent him happily on his way. Before the end of the week, the solicitor had brought to his church two new families who, unknown to the minister, had been living in the community for several months. The salesman had discovered them in his house-to-house canvass.

TIME MUST BE SCHEDULED

Many a clergyman is discouraged when he attempts to schedule his time. He finds himself without definite bidding from others; he seems unable to direct himself. Perhaps he realizes his difficulty and makes a program for himself. Emergencies arise, his schedule is disrupted and he neglects to restore it. Before he realizes it, he is likely to find himself just " puttering around," until his habits of energetic study, office work, parish routine and general efficiency are shattered and gone.

Just as the heads of families in his church maintain daily schedules of work for themselves, so the minister should establish for himself a rigid discipline. To illustrate this point I quote from a minister in Michigan:

" I left the seminary in 1921 and have been in business in various capacities since.

" As I look back, I believe that while there were several strong reasons for my leaving the ministry, the step might have been averted at least for some years, and possibly avoided entirely, had I known better how to use my time.

" Since going into business, I have been impressed with the fact that office and factory employees are required to make good use of the business hours of the day, and that successful businessmen are invariably those who combine with other qualities this essential — that they decide wisely on how to use every moment of their time and make themselves carry out their decisions.

" There may not be much lost when a real-estate salesman who did not know how to use his time turns to clerking in a store, but something is lost when a minister with a theological training, which for the most part he did not provide himself, but for which he is indebted to the church that gave it to him, turns into an ordinary clerk.

" And is there anything supernatural or extraordinary in the minister's make-up, or in his inspiration, which gives him the ability that other classes of men must develop through long years of discipline? "

THE WORKING DAY

The question is often asked, how long should a minister's working day be? Would it not be fair to say that as a rule the length of the minister's day should be about the same as that of the average member of his congregation? The city minister, for instance, who must work under high mental pressure, with many brief but intensive interviews and large groups of interests, may need to adopt habits of work entirely different from those of the man in the mining town or in the country parish.

Some ministers do not know how to analyze their duties for the purpose of scheduling. They do not seem to know when their working day should begin or end. Their work is never done, and their day is never long enough. They cannot feel the joys of finished tasks.

Let us imagine that the habits of the community warrant the minister's planning his work for an eight-hour day. He should guard those eight hours, and confine them to the interests of the church as strictly as though he were an employee of a large business establishment. There is no time here for personal errands or idle conversation or miscellaneous reading. These may be permitted outside of his working hours.

If definite hours are set aside for one's office, they should not be confined to " catching up on the work."

It might be better to clear everything off the desk, tables and shelves and to put it all in the wastebasket, and then, with a fresh mental attitude, begin the planning of a new and more vital program for the church.

A story is told of John D. Rockefeller when in his younger days he was beginning to be recognized as a powerful man. His great company at that time was organized as a single unit with managers in many different cities.

In one of the offices, it is reported, he visited an executive whose desk was piled high with papers of various kinds. The man apologized by saying that he had been crowded and exceedingly busy; " but I'll manage to get through with it all," he added.

According to the story, Mr. Rockefeller replied: " I want the men who have charge of the different branches of my business to have time to put their feet up, lean back, and think of new ways to make money for Standard Oil."

In the daily hours of planning, just as during his time for prayers, there should come to the minister the picture of his whole church — its strength and its weakness. With the aid of this larger view he is able to provide for commendation of work well done, and make plans to strengthen the weak places. With his entire organization in mind, the minister should first relate it to the community; then he should think in terms of his denomination, of which his parish and his work are an important part; after which he should consider the nation and the world, with their needs, and the things his church could do to help to meet these greater needs.

Who knows but that a great leader may be in the making

in his congregation? There is work of a world-wide nature for every church to do. A vision of this kind makes the day all too short, and reveals plenty of reasons for definitely necessary calls at offices and homes.

Then follows the communication of this vision to the people. Suppose the minister devotes his afternoon to pastoral calls, giving half his time to old business and half to new; half to calls of good cheer, counsel and encouragement, half to seeking new members and workers for the church. Let him perform this part of his work as conscientiously and keep track of it as carefully as though he must report each call with its results to his board of trustees, just as must be done by many a salesman for the business firm he represents.

Is it not clear that such a schedule would bring good results?

SCHEDULING FOR SELF-PROTECTION

How shall a minister protect himself against unwelcome calls for service? Dr. Bernard C. Clausen, in his book *The Technique of a Minister* (Revell), tells how clergymen so often become " slaves of a desk pad," promising almost any service in response to telephone or other appeals, provided the space is clear on their engagement books. He recommends, not keeping the desk pad clear in the expectation of such calls, but filling it as far as desired with the minister's own engagements. The minister's day of rest or of recreation, for example, is always scheduled in advance. He must not list other engagements for that day, any more than he would break appointments with members of his church for his personal benefit. He must consider it a moral obligation to save certain hours for himself and his family.

How far should a minister plan ahead? It would seem that he ought to look forward at least a year. Those who follow the church year have a better opportunity than others to plan their sermons in advance, but almost every minister can see ahead for twelve months.

At the Chicago Theological Seminary, we find it helpful to work on several schedules. First, there is a three-year program, based on the seminary's triennial convention as a source of authority and responsibility. Next, there is an annual outline governed by the seminary's academic and financial needs. This involves curricula, budgets, campaigns of promotion and reports to the board of directors. Then there are: the monthly program headed by the executive committee; the weekly faculty sessions; and, perhaps most important, the daily program, which is outlined and carried out conscientiously, because if tasks are left unfinished they accumulate and become a burden. Keeping all of these schedules harmonized in one's mind makes it natural to carry them out completely and without confusion, since each one supplements the others.

Fortunate is that minister who can get people into the habit of coming to him instead of his having to visit them.

The social life of the church need not center in the minister's home, provided he is wise enough to group it around the leaders of the church. This applies to financial, publicity, and all other departments of church work as well, except the spiritual leadership, for which a pastor should count himself primarily responsible.

Sometimes when a minister has much to do, and finds it difficult to determine what is most important, he might just begin on the items nearest at hand. Clear them away, one by one. Keep a note pad near. Suggestions will come frequently from the subconscious mind. Write them down. Do not get sidetracked on the consideration of the many indirect suggestions, but make a record of them; they are valuable. Then take up the new suggestions, analyze them, plan ahead, and you will experience the joys of creative thought.

Many of us work too hard. We " promote " too much. We drive our associates into confusion, forgetting that the true shepherd leads his flock to green pastures and cooling drink, and then rests with them in quiet fellowship; and they feel satisfied and secure because their shepherd is near them and they trust his leadership.

There is time for everything that needs to be done. Is the minister's day too short? Then it is time, not to work harder, but to relax, and think and pray. There is a solution to every problem. Often the lesson is learned only after a nervous breakdown or a forced rest, but this is hardly the best way. In a time of storm at sea, when the disciples were sorely troubled, Jesus arose and said, " Peace, be still! . . . and there was a great calm," — and the disciples were refreshed and went forward to new achievements.

Chapter Ten

PERSONAL CONDUCT

THE STAGE was all set for the calling of a new minister. The congregation was larger than usual, and the people were expectant. The young man from the seminary preached one of his best sermons and went home that day with hope in his heart; but he did not receive the call. He never knew why, but the pulpit committee told me that it was because when he was seated on the platform he crossed one knee over the other, and as he nervously dangled his foot they were annoyed by " the dazzle of his striped socks."

Not long ago I was shown through a great citrus packing plant in the South by one of my minister friends. Here the oranges and grapefruit from nearby orchards were brought in by wagonloads, dumped into washing vats, scrubbed, paraffined, and carried forward on long revolving belts for inspection; then they were automatically sorted into bins and were soon ready for crating, so many to the box. It was a fascinating process to watch.

The imperfect fruit, taken from the moving belts, is called " culls."

My friend was well received, and so, on his account, was I. We were introduced to the managers of the plant who respectfully addressed us as they thought fitting when speaking to " doctors of divinity."

As we were ready to leave, my friend inquired of the fore-

man as to the number of " culls " on hand. Being told that
there was a surplus, he asked if he might have a bushel of
them. His request was granted, and shortly afterward he
walked happily out of the packing plant with a large im-
provised bag of culls in his arms.

I had never been more chagrined in my life. What had
happened? The " doctors of divinity," by selfishly asking
for free inferior fruit, had classed themselves with the culls
in the laymen's mind. I do not consider such action good
business; and yet, in one form or another, such practices
are more or less common among pastors. And then they
wonder what is wrong with their laymen! Far rather would
I have bought a box of the highest grade of fruit as a gift for
my friend than to have suffered this humiliation. Having
done so, I would have been perfectly willing to go later with
my friend to the managers of the plant to seek a generous
contribution for the program of his church.

This same minister is preaching free of charge in a vacant
pulpit with the hope that, in the course of time, the people
will employ him permanently. But I doubt that he will receive the call, for human nature is such that it does not value
that for which it does not pay.

A young minister applied to me for help in securing a
clergy permit for railroad transportation to which he was not
entitled, desiring to take advantage of possible reduced rates
for his personal benefit rather than for the service of the
church. I did not feel that this was best for the cause, and I
advised him against making the application, but " he went
away sorrowful."

THE FACTOR OF PERSONALITY

A minister's preaching may be above reproach, and yet his influence in the community may be so undermined by his personal conduct that his days are filled with discouragement and his work ends in failure.

No position among the professions requires such tact and diplomacy as that of the ministry. Just as a salesman is rewarded in business by his power to adapt his personality to those with whom he comes in contact, so the minister's success in the work of his parish may depend upon his ability so to conduct himself that in his daily living he will win the respect, confidence and cooperation of his congregation.

A minister should remember that he comes to a new community as a man of God. He is not considered an ordinary person. Will he make himself common by a slovenly walk, an unkempt appearance and a carelessness of speech which will rob him of his influence? Will he show his temper under provocation, become confused by emergencies, display a lack of courage in time of opposition? Will he seek praise or sympathy for himself? Will he resent criticism and advice? Will he forget the dignity of his position as a Christian gentleman and an ambassador of the church universal? Then he is not yet a real leader and his people will soon discover it.

A minister should be sincere not only in the preparation and delivery of his sermons, but in his pastoral duties and in the business organization of the church. If he is honest, his congregation will forgive much that he may lack. A woman who had been an invalid for many years remarked to her daughter, " I wish the minister would not call any more, for he does not seem sincere." How sensitive is such a sufferer in discerning whether or not her spiritual adviser has come with a true message of cheer, or simply to cover the list and compile his denominational statistics.

Some ministers think that their time is too valuable to do what they term "errand boy work" in making pastoral calls. It should be remembered that many of our Savior's greatest sermons were delivered to individuals, and that his preaching to the multitudes did not compare in importance with the training and the organization of his little groups of from three to twelve.

A good rule to observe in calling at either homes or offices is to prepare in advance, as points of contact, definite reasons for the calls. This principle applies also to the writing of letters. Miscellaneous calling or correspondence leads to no definite goal and should not find place in a busy pastor's schedule.

FINANCIAL OBLIGATIONS

A minister should meet his financial obligations punctually. If, because of sickness or adversity, this seems impossible, then he should go frankly to those involved, explain the situation, and make such adjustments as may be necessary or desired. Many a congregation suffers humiliation in the community because of the carelessness and the neglect of its minister to pay his accounts as they fall due. It is almost proverbial that clergymen are careless in this respect. The minister may take the attitude that his income is insufficient to meet his needs. This does not excuse him in the minds of the merchants, who are likely to feel that he is not worth as much as he gets. As a result of having established a basis of questionable conduct, the minister is unlikely to receive larger financial recognition and his place of leadership will become increasingly insecure.

Numerous worthy ministers with high business ideals have been handicapped in their work because of the imprudence of their predecessors in habits of personal finance. It is reported that in a certain Ohio city a minister left town with so many debts that the trustees of the church made a specific contract with the newly called man, providing that on the first day of every month he would receive his salary in advance on condition that he would agree to pay cash for everything that he purchased. Should he break this rule and begin running charge accounts, his contract automatically would be canceled. This new minister's character may have entitled him to a financial rating as high as that of any businessman, but he had to bear the disgrace that had come to his church through the misconduct of the former pastor.

Another minister of my acquaintance has been trying unsuccessfully for more than five years to secure a new location. Several churches have been interested in him, for he is a strong preacher and a man of excellent qualities, but he has not received a call. I doubt if he knows that the reason is the unsavory financial record he left behind him in his previous parish.

LOANS AND DISCOUNTS

If a minister feels that he must borrow money, he should seek it at the bank or through other business channels rather than from his friends. If his credit is not good he should not borrow. It would be better by far for him to adjust his personal budget.

Notwithstanding the seeming benefits, the prevailing tendency to seek discounts and other similar gratuities at the stores should be discouraged. The pastor who must have discounts to live is likely to become a discounted man in his community. The higher ethics of business recognize the fairness of one price to all — it being understood that on this basis, with the increased income from his business, there is nothing to prevent the doctor, the butcher, the grocer or the clothier from making a more generous subscription to the church, a subscription which in turn may revert to the minister.

I wish more of our pastors could realize what businessmen think of their methods of securing passes, free entertainment and other privileges for personal profit or advantage which have come to be known as " preachers' graft."

Where gratuities are offered voluntarily, without the expectation of personal obligation or return, a clergyman may feel free to accept them. Many business firms grant these favors as gifts to the church rather than to the representative of the pulpit, and it would seem tactless, if not unwise, to deny them this privilege.

A minister should not attempt to be a jack-of-all-trades. The less he seems to know about the material side of the church, the better, provided he can organize his forces and delegate the responsibilities to others. It is a mistake for him to try to be church electrician, carpenter, decorator, plumber and general handy man. I knew one young pastor who was so useful in all of these things that he really became an assistant to the janitor and thereby lost his prestige as the executive leader of the church.

DANGERS OF SIDE LINES

The minister who wishes to be successful should beware of taking on questionable side lines to increase his income. There are certain legitimate supplemental services which a minister may render, such as the delivery of public addresses or the writing of appropriate articles or books for publication. Such activities help to make him and his work better known, and they multiply his usefulness to an ever enlarging constituency. But when a pastor enters the realm of business and adds to his work unrelated interests, such as the selling of books, merchandise or insurance, or the managing of other institutions, like the local chamber of commerce, then he is doing nothing less than serving two masters, neither of whom he will be able to satisfy.

A young minister should be willing to give certain years of his early service at a nominal salary, during which time he may increase his initiative, mature his judgment and enrich his experience, just as the businessman must go through years of struggle in his work before he may expect an adequate reward for his labors. A young businessman who would turn aside from his purpose to supplement his income with a side line must give up his hope of leadership. If a side line seems necessary, then let it become the main line.

Some ministers accept personal benefits, such as free sets of books or gifts of stock, in return for endorsements or lists of names or other favors which they have no right to sell. Such practices are not advisable, for they weaken the influence of both the minister and the church.

THE SNARES OF INVESTMENT

Great care should be used in making personal investments. Considerable study has been given to the subject of why ministers are on the so-called " sucker list " of blue-sky promoters. It is comparatively easy for a good salesman to sell securities to a clergyman, whether the investment is good or bad. This is due largely to the minister's unfamiliarity with questions of finance. Concerning this subject, a letter once came to me from a clergyman saying: " Warn the young men to beware of oil stocks, mining stocks, real estate and similar investments, that they may not get caught, as have been most of us who were without experience." An investment which pays more than a conservative rate of interest is generally speculative, and a minister's hard-earned money should not be risked unnecessarily.

Pastors, of course, are not the only individuals who make mistakes in financial investments. An interesting sidelight, from a clergyman's standpoint, is the statement of a prominent pastor who says that " ministers are often criticized because of their wildcat investments in business enterprises, while bankers and others are just as foolish in making their investments in wildcat benevolences. Businessmen receive appeals from various schools and charitable enterprises, to which they often contribute generously without consulting their pastors or others who might be in a position to give expert advice."

Shall a minister buy merchandise from a mail order house? Why not? Has he not the same privileges as his neighbor? And yet, there is the other side; in the case of the minister it may be " good business " to build up, through buying in local stores, the community that supports him and makes possible the development of his work. In fact, it might become embarrassing to seek either financial cooperation or volunteer service from those in one's congregation whose business services one has neglected in favor of outside concerns.

Men of the calling should guard against a tendency to roughness in their bearing. I like to think of " the gentle Jesus." They should avoid slang and be courteous and gracious to all men, including those of their own households. A true gentleman does not have different sets of manners for home, street and pulpit. They are all one.

Appointments and promises should be kept diligently.

PERSONAL APPEARANCE

As to questions of dress and personal appearance, I quote a prominent pastor who spent several days at a leading seminary and, with a desire to help them in their problems, interviewed students who were about to graduate. In the report of his visit he included these comments:

" It was noticeable that some of the students were having a hard time to make ends meet. No doubt, however, when they blossom out in their Sunday clothes, they appear quite different. I wish, however, that more of them would realize that an every-morning shave and shine, pressed trousers, clean clothes and linens have a strong bearing upon one's self-respect and the esteem of others. This may seem a simple suggestion, but it is indisputable that good appearance is an asset in one's work. The dignity of one's bearing adds materially to his ability in both pulpit and parish. The members of the church do not fail to see whether or not the min-

6093

ister is well dressed and well groomed, or slovenly in his personal habits. Many people feel that an immaculate appearance is symbolic of the spiritual life and thought within. As a minister of God, one ought to be at his best in his daily life and work."

A minister should keep physically fit. He has no right to mortgage either his present or his future by burning his candle at both ends. Not long ago a call was issued for volunteers "to burn out for God" in a certain mission field. This was a false conception of one's largest service to the church.

A tired body means a poor imagination, impatience and defective judgment. It handicaps the memory. It discounts efficiency and it takes away the joy of one's achievements.

The Christian ministry is the greatest calling in the world. As a layman in other lines of work, I have met ministers in their homes in cities large and small. I have worshiped with them in their churches. I have attended conventions and conferences. I know them from several points of view, and they are wonderful men. But somehow it makes me sad when I find many of them thinking that they must be " regular fellows," like other men. Deep down in my heart, I want them to be different. I long for them to be holy men as Jesus was!

There are four great words in the destiny of man: Life, death, God and love. " Meditate upon these things; give thyself wholly to them; that thy profiting may appear to all " (I Tim. 4:15).

Chapter Eleven

THE CARE OF CHURCH PROPERTY

I had rather be a doorkeeper in the house of my God, than to dwell in the tents of wickedness.

PS. 84:10

MOST CHURCHES and other religious institutions were well conceived and built because of the high ideals and the sacrificial gifts of their founders. For most of them good architects were employed, and the best of materials were used in construction. But it would appear in many churches that, after the day of the dedication, the task of preservation is almost entirely neglected.

Automobiles and machinery need care; office buildings and stores require constant attention to continue to operate efficiently and profitably; but how many church budgets include appropriations sufficient to keep their buildings and equipment up to their original standard, so that, as with the cathedrals of Europe, age adds only to their beauty and increases the rich memories of bygone days?

It hurts our inner sensitiveness to see the magazine cartoons of "the little brown church at the crossroads," with cobwebs on the windows and everything in decay. Somebody must have loved that church when it was founded; christenings, weddings and services of worship have hallowed it; mourners have gathered there to pay their last tributes to the dead and to hope for life eternal. It does not deserve to be neglected.

Who of us has not felt a twinge of disappointment, if not of shame, when we have seen a church with treeless and unkempt yards, broken walks, cracked windows, unpointed stones and brick, or with walls and woodwork last painted in a time beyond remembrance.

And as we entered, perhaps for worship, was not our attention distracted by cracks in the plaster and stains from leaky roofs? Did we reach for a ragged hymnbook in a pew rack that was loose? Were there dead or missing lamps and worn out fixtures? Were the carpets torn? Were the floors and the furniture in poor repair?

But wait, let us go into the basement, where children gather for their classes and where suppers and banquets are held. What is the condition of the walls and their decoration? What are the facilities for fresh drinking water? Are the windows clean, the pianos in tune? Are there hooks for coats and hats at a height that can be reached by the children? Are the closets and storerooms in order? What about the washrooms and the toilets? Are they well equipped and sanitary?

THE CHURCH ENTRANCE

And the entrance to the church. Is it friendly? Does it seem to say " Come in "? Must one first go up a flight of steps which perhaps in the winter is covered with ice and snow? Are the outside bulletin boards fresh and clean, or are they shabby and out of date? Is there a sign at the door to announce the name of the church and the pastor, and a schedule of the services within?

As I pass in and out of gloomy church halls, I think often of the entrances to our motion picture theaters. I have no doubts there as to my welcome. Illuminated signs bearing the name of the institution and the chief features of the program greet me from afar. As I approach the doors, photographs and colored posters tempt me to go within.

I wonder if there are not lessons here for the church!

" I was driving in the country one Sunday evening," said a friend, " with a sincere desire to attend a church. Suddenly, at the edge of a small town, I came to a building which had the appearance of a place of worship. There was no sign on it to indicate the denomination or the hours of service. A steep flight of steps led up to a dimly lighted vestibule. The whole atmosphere was so gloomy and depressing that I had not the courage to go in."

WHAT THE PARSONAGE MAY REVEAL

When campaigning for the new buildings of the Chicago Theological Seminary, I visited all of the churches of our denomination in the Chicago area.

A few miles from the city, there was a little white church on the side of the hill, and some distance away was the parsonage. As I approached this home I could scarcely believe that it was occupied. There were tall weeds in the yard, several windows were cracked or broken, some of the screens were rusted away in their frames and the front gate was hanging on one hinge.

When I saw the outside of the house I did not enter, for I knew that no minister who so neglected his home could be of any help among businessmen in a financial campaign. I made inquiries, however, from some of the neighboring farmers, and found that they had long since withdrawn their support of this man because of his shiftless methods of living. I was not surprised, a few weeks later, to learn that he had lost his position.

There is a congregation in Wisconsin which not only prides itself on the upkeep of its church property, but which has adopted a ten-year progressive program of improvement. A leading architect has been consulted, and each step leads to the next, until a completed and harmonious plan will have been fulfilled.

A FIRST STEP IN RAISING MONEY

In a certain Chicago church I was elected chairman of the board of trustees. The budget of the church was sixteen thousand dollars, and there was a deficit of three thousand dollars which I was expected to raise by some magic. I took inventory. The properties were run down and the people were discouraged. I knew that the money could not be secured unless the people could be convinced that we were " under new management." Before attempting any campaign we began an extensive program of repairs and renewals. The leaks of the roof were stopped, the window frames calked, the masonry pointed, the woodwork painted, the furnace was cleaned, the lighting improved, the radiator valves and traps adjusted, broken glass replaced, and the church rooms throughout the buildings were renovated. Trees were trimmed and grass and flowers planted in the yards. Special attention was given to the kindergarten and primary rooms, where new linoleum, curtains, wallpaper and gaily painted chairs were furnished to brighten the formerly dingy atmosphere. When we had finished, our deficit had been increased from three thousand dollars to six thousand dollars, but there was a different spirit in the congregation.

Then I began a financial campaign by mail, based on the slogan " Make me a little cake first," as told in I Kings 17:13, where Elijah approached the starving widow who was ready to prepare her last meal before dying; and the story reveals that " she went and did according to the saying of Elijah, and the barrel of meal wasted not, and neither did the cruse of oil fail."

And so it was with this church. Sixty-five hundred dollars was raised. Best of all, the neighbors caught our spirit and began to paint and improve their properties, so that the whole community was raised to a new level of civic consciousness.

Let us turn to another church. I had lunch recently with the key layman of the church — a quiet, modest Christian gentleman. He had suffered heavy financial losses in the recent depression. I did not think he could be approached for additional gifts. He began telling me of the new improvements he was responsible for in the church buildings: the organ had been repaired, new furniture had been purchased for the minister's office, etc. Finally he asked, " Wouldn't you like to see what I have done? " " Certainly," I replied, and we went together to inspect the work. The massive roof had been rebuilt, the stonework pointed, new doors installed, and new carpets had been laid throughout the buildings. It was a generous restoration. My friend said, " It cost me ninety-seven thousand dollars, but now I can sleep at night."

CASTING BREAD UPON THE WATERS

Some of us may say, " Surely, all this can be done if you have the money." But I shall reply with the testimony of a Nebraska minister that " it makes money for the church. . . . Your suggestion of cleaning up our church property," he continues, " and of giving the buildings a new coat of paint inside and out, planting a lawn and making various other physical improvements has worked wonders for our church. It has not only enlarged our attendance, but it has increased our financial support."

During the years of depression, we have observed that the stores, hotels, apartment buildings, railroads and other business enterprises which have kept in the lead are those which have modernized their properties and have made them attractive to the public.

Ministers, would you have new and larger buildings or equipment entrusted to your care? Then guard well your present commitments.

In Luke 8:18 we read: " For whosoever hath, to him shall be given; and whosoever hath not, from him shall be taken even that which he seemeth to have." As related to institutional property, I should like to interpret this to read: " For whosoever taketh care of what he hath, to him shall more be given; but whosoever taketh not care of what he hath, from him shall even that which he hath be taken away." Is it not a question of Christian stewardship?

TAKING CARE OF WHAT YOU HAVE

In one church, I saw the holy Bible lying on a dusty floor, where it had been carelessly thrown to make way for a more modern version. Even though not in use, this Bible might have been placed on a mahogany table with a velvet covering. In another church I noticed a large pulpit Bible sadly in need of rebinding. It had been given as a memorial in 1875. I looked at the inscription and asked the pastor:

" Is this woman living? "

" No," he replied, " she is dead."

" Are her children living? "

" Yes, they are members of this church."

" Why not ask them to restore their mother's gift? " I suggested.

And he answered, " I never thought of that."

As we look about, we can see almost countless opportunities for the beautification of our church properties. For example:

Improve the lawns, trees, shrubs and flower beds.

Remove unsightly buildings and rubbish from the yards.

Provide appropriate pictures for the halls, parlors and classrooms.

Put velvet or other suitable coverings over the chancel furniture.

Supply small, bright-colored tables, chairs and other needed furniture and equipment for the beginners and primary departments.

Help the minister to make his office a model of physical comfort and business efficiency.

See that good signs and attractive bulletin boards are installed, as needed.

Keep the hymnbooks repaired, and arranged in orderly fashion in the pew racks.

Remove all glaring lights and modernize their fixtures.

Put carpets on the platform and in the aisles.

Keep the buildings clean, decorated and in good repair.

If the regular church budget does not cover these items, most of them can be provided as projects by special groups, or as memorials from interested friends, so that we may repeat sincerely the psalmist's words: " I was glad when they said unto me, Let us go into the house of the Lord."

CHURCH MAY SET CIVIC EXAMPLE

A few years ago it was my privilege to be present at the meeting of the National Council of Congregational Churches in Detroit, when the Reverend Jesse Perrin, a senior student of the Chicago Theological Seminary, gave a report of his summer service at Hermosa, South Dakota, as a representative of the Church Extension Society. Among other things, he said:

" The town to which I was sent proved to be a ' has-been.' It had been a freighting point for the mining operations in the heart of the Black hills.

" In its glory it had boasted eleven saloons and three churches; but the railroad was extended, and the town was left to die, saloons, churches and all. Now it has only seventy-five inhabitants, two small stores, a bank, a post office, a garage and a small hotel, and about three blocks of empty buildings.

" The town had been without any Protestant services for nearly a year. The people thought they were too poor to support a church, and indeed they were poor in material things but wonderfully rich in spiritual gifts.

" Twelve people came to church that first Sunday, but as the weeks went by the church shook itself free from inertia and began to do things. A choir was organized, socials were held and a Fourth of July picnic, and people began to come to church.

" The summer was half gone when I made the remark that I would be glad to paint the thirty year old parsonage, which had never known the warmth of a coat of paint, if only the money could be raised to purchase the necessary supplies. One man who heard me was a trustee, and the next Sunday after church he raised the needed forty dollars. I set to work, and the parsonage on the hill soon shone with three coats of white paint.

" But Satan was not to be outdone by the Lord. The proprietor of the pool hall fell in with the spirit of the preacher and painted his building; so also did the hardware man. Later the garage man and the hotelkeeper did likewise. The whole town began to take on more civic pride. A sign was put on the church where all passers-by could read it, and we were very proud of our achievements.

" During the third summer the church decided to enlarge its plant. Everybody helped. It was a cooperative community enterprise, and ended in a homemade church building, with kitchen, recreation room and all.

" We had a shingling bee one day, when thirty farmers worked on the roof and grounds, getting the building ready for the final touch of the plasterer and the painter.

" And as we joyfully laid shingles that day, we little dreamed that two years later the President of the United States would choose to worship under that humble roof, in preference to other places that had been prepared for him."

Would we be ready, as Jesse Perrin was, if a similar experience should come to us?

CHAPTER TWELVE

CONVENTIONS, CONFERENCES AND SPECIAL MEETINGS

HOW TO INVITE, SUPERVISE AND ENTERTAIN THEM

"LET US sing hymn number 340," announced the leader of devotions at a state conference of churches; but there was no response from the organ.

" I see we have no organist," he said. " Will anybody volunteer to play for us? " There was no volunteer. The hymn was sung in the wrong key, without accompaniment, and the conference began its program in a gloomy atmosphere.

At another convention of five hundred delegates, a stirring appeal was made for the old age pensions of retired ministers. Every man present was reaching for his pocketbook when the chairman asked:

" Will the ushers come forward to take the offering? "

No ushers had been appointed.

The chairman then selected ushers from the floor. They came forward, but no collection plates could be found.

The chairman was so embarrassed that he said, " We will dispense with the offering until the afternoon session."

Later, when the contributions were finally taken, the inspiration was gone and many of the delegates had left. The offering was noticeably small.

The frequency of such incidents justifies a rather detailed

treatment, addressed to ministers and laymen alike, of convention management.

For the purpose of simplification the word " convention " will be used to cover all meetings at which delegates may be present from outside the local organization.

There are at least five good reasons for holding conventions:

(1) To provide Christian fellowship and the exchange of general information.

(2) To define the policies and create the desired program of the movement involved.

(3) To cultivate the friendship of the individual and acquaint him with the purposes of the organization.

(4) To produce a loyal constituency for the program to be promoted.

(5) To establish a clearinghouse for new ideas, so that the work may grow rapidly.

We are all familiar with the national propaganda campaigns to encourage the patronizing of one's neighborhood grocer or druggist. The corner drugstore has been changed in a single generation from an old-fashioned pharmacy to a modern community center. The popularizing of a neighborhood drugstore pays, from a financial standpoint. The more people visit the store, even for postage stamps, newspapers or telephone service or to wait for the street car, the better it is for the business.

Would it not also be true of the church? Many a building is locked up tightly from one Sunday to another, and then is open mostly for its own church family.

Properly managed conventions will make a church stand

out in its community and will popularize it to such an extent that both the minister and his people are counted an asset to their town or city.

Our subject naturally divides itself into two parts: (1) the convention invitation; (2) the promotion and supervision of conventions.

THE CONVENTION INVITATION

Every minister should try to secure for his church as many as possible of the right kind of meetings, such as denominational conferences — county, state and national; association meetings; missionary rallies; church school and Christian Endeavor conventions, etc.

The minister should seek especially meetings of a religious-educational nature, for the reason that if such groups are properly entertained by his congregation the whole program of his church will be uplifted, the work will grow, and a new spirit of enthusiasm and earnestness will soon reveal itself.

Not all churches can entertain the larger meetings, but every church should invite some outside organizations to share its fellowship.

When considering the invitation to a convention, the minister should keep in mind several requirements, for example:

Location. Are the town and church easy to reach?

Transportation. What are the methods of travel, and are the time schedules convenient for those who will attend?

Buildings. Can adequate rooms be furnished for the major sessions and for the smaller conferences, committee meetings and exhibits? (Sometimes several neighboring churches may cooperate to meet such needs.)

Entertainment. The question of hotels, or rooms and meals in private homes, is important.

Publicity. Will the local press cooperate? The religious papers?

Local committee. Perhaps the essentials for success are the organization, the spirit and the enthusiastic support of this committee, without which no convention can hope to succeed.

If these six items can be covered satisfactorily, then the church is ready to extend its invitations.

Usually there is competition in securing the better class of conventions, and it is wise to be represented at the previous meeting of the organization by a strong promotion committee whose members will be prepared to set forth the advantages of the proposed convention church and town or city, and who should be able to speak with authority regarding such financial and other items as may be involved. Letters or telegrams read at the proper times from the church board, the ministers' union, the association of commerce, the mayor, the Rotary Club and other well known officials and organizations are helpful in creating favorable sentiment. Photographs and other exhibits of the convention church and city are also helpful. Likewise, attractive slogans displayed on banners, buttons or cards, and the distribution of good advertising literature have their influence.

When once the promise of the convention is secured, even though it may be a year or more in advance of the meeting, it is none too early to take advantage of every possible item of publicity and to begin a preliminary organization of the forces which will be needed for its entertainment.

PROMOTION AND SUPERVISION OF CONVENTIONS

Now let us turn from the local church and town or city to the larger consideration of conventions as a whole, regardless of whether the minister is entertaining a convention himself, or holding responsibilities of convention management in other places. Suppose that suddenly the minister or one of his laymen is called upon to be responsible for the promotion of a county, state, national, or even a world-wide organization. What shall he do? How shall he begin?

As in the case of financial campaigns and church organization, it cannot be too strongly emphasized that if one expects to succeed in the promotion of conventions he must be able to dream and think out the entire program in advance. Many men are able to do this months and years ahead. Marion Lawrance, for many years the general secretary of the World's and International Sunday School associations, planned his conventions four years ahead. Of course, he did not organize the local committees or issue literature or inform the public so long in advance, but everything was clear in his own mind.

A successful convention depends very largely upon keen conception, advance planning, capable promotion and expert management.

As a test of preparedness I often ask myself, " What would I do if all that I have planned should fail? " And having found the answer, I ask again, " Suppose this too should fail? " By repeating this process until I am sure of myself should any eventuality befall, I am then ready to proceed.

Annual meetings should be planned rather definitely three months ahead of the scheduled date and should be fairly well organized one month before the meeting opens.

No convention should be called which does not have back of it a worthy purpose. A high goal will naturally develop a theme, and this theme may become the basis of the advertising and publicity.

When the date of the convention is determined, it is desirable to make certain, if possible, that the meeting will have the right of way in the convention city. This should be done through the influence of the local committee. Other competitive assemblies might lessen the influence of the convention, no matter how well it may be organized.

From a promotion standpoint, first will come the official call; next, the announcements and bulletins to prospective delegates; and then follow correspondence, advertising and publicity.

It is desirable to keep in close personal touch with each prospective delegate, so that his interest may be increased and his attendance assured. He should be informed of the convention in advance and as fully as possible. Maps, routes of travel, information about the meetings and their leaders and speakers, recreation, banquets, etc., as well as bulletins on the subjects likely to be considered at the business sessions may be sent to him for this purpose.

Each delegate should receive a program before the convention opens, and this should be sent to him with a personal letter from the president or chairman.

All advance information should be of an inspirational nature, full of enthusiasm, anticipation and forcefulness, and not merely an outline of the facts. A study of type of promotion on the airline, railroad and steamship circulars which are designed to create the desire for travel will illustrate this point.

Attendance at the convention should never be intimated to be a duty, but rather an opportunity. Investments of time and money, rather than the cost, should be stressed.

For conventions of one hundred delegates or more, there are five major committees to be organized — those to deal with the program, transportation, finance, invitation (or attendance), and finally a local committee on arrangements.

For larger conventions, subcommittees may be added to attend to such matters as reception, registration, entertainment, ushers, banquet, exhibits, first aid, decoration, music, publicity, recreation, pulpit supply, information, dramatization, parade, supplies, audit, conservation. There should also be a bureau of complaints.

While the organization should be comprehensive enough to cover all needs, it is well to keep it as simple as possible to meet the requirements.

For more than twenty-five years I have been involved in the promotion of conventions, some of them at home and others abroad; some with dozens in attendance, others with thousands. Without experience it is difficult for one to comprehend the intricacies of the convention system, yet inspiration and personal benefit as well as the satisfactions of altruistic service come from the successful administration of the larger gatherings.

PROGRAM BUILDING

In building the program, one should be careful to choose the right speakers to develop the convention purpose, rather than try to group the topics around certain well known available leaders. I remember one great convention which had so many prominent speakers from outside organizations on its program that the purpose of the meeting was not developed and the investment in promotion was almost lost.

The program should be built toward a climax. The strongest speakers and the best entertainment should be placed near the end, to avoid an anticlimax and its attendant discouraging falling-off of interest and attendance.

At many conventions attendance at either the opening or closing sessions is considered by the delegates scarcely worth while. This fault in program arrangement could be avoided through careful planning and thorough advance promotion.

The program should be balanced so as to have a proper adjustment of the inspirational features with those of business and entertainment.

What are known as " steam-roller " and " rubber-stamp " methods promoted by the " inner ring " should be avoided lest opposition and friction develop and the benefits of the convention be diminished. One of the best ways to prevent the possibility of such methods is to allow time for conferences and discussion and to arrange for as many people as possible to take part. " I have just attended a wonderful convention," said the happy delegate as he returned home. " I made a speech," he added, and thereby revealed the secret of a successful meeting.

Differences of opinion should be kept out of public sessions. Refer them to subcommittees for study, compromise and later report. Eliminate all favoritisms, prejudices and personalities.

The duties of the presiding officer of a convention will include:

Calling the meetings to order.

Making certain that a quorum is present at a business session.

Stating all regular motions.

Telling the results of votes.

Preserving order in debate.

Recognizing the rights of the floor.

Defending points of order.

Seeing that the rules of the meeting are carried out.

A secretary should be appointed at the opening service who will remain through all of the sessions and record the actions taken. He will read the minutes of the previous meeting when requested by the chair, and will present such resolutions as may be placed in his hands by the proper committees. He will count the votes, preserve the documents, notify officers and committees of their appointments, and complete the minutes of the assembly.

Do not overcrowd the program. Two leading speakers to a session are enough; one is better. Appropriate music is important.

Business meetings may be listed for the morning; departmental conferences and recreation for the afternoon; and inspirational sessions for night.

The program should move forward as scheduled. This is possible if the right president or chairman is in charge.

In selecting speakers, one should bear in mind two points of equal importance: (1) Those who have something to say; (2) those who know how to say it.

Written agreements should be made in advance with each participant, covering the time, place and length of the addresses to be given, and the honorarium and expenses to be paid.

A marked copy of the program should be sent in advance to each speaker.

PROBLEMS OF TRANSPORTATION

The duties of the transportation committee are important but usually not difficult, the responsibilities depending somewhat upon the size of the convention to be held and the geographical territory to be covered.

A local association meeting, for example, may involve only passage on street cars, automobiles and buses, while a world convention may call for special trains, airplanes and chartered ships, thereby requiring the utmost skill and leadership by members of the transportation committee to meet the difficult situations which are certain to arise.

The transportation committee will seek to find the most pleasant routes and modes of travel; issue maps, bulletins and baggage tags; and secure agreements for reduced rates on buses, trains and ships, when possible.

A transportation committee that can deliver its delegates at the convention, take care of them during the meetings and get them safely home again has made its place in history.

THE FINANCE COMMITTEE

A convention is always more welcome and successful, if the question of finance can be covered quietly and efficiently in advance. A convention deficit is almost a calamity.

The finance committee will make up its budget from a study of previous records and from a knowledge of the new requirements which will be presented by the program committee. It will supervise the receipt of fees and various other funds, pay the bills, and see that the expenses of the meeting remain within the budget.

Sometimes the purchase of supplies is referred also to the finance committee. These may include blackboards, note-books, stationery, badges, signs, banners, souvenirs, etc.

A convention may be financed from the budget of the organization it represents, or by dues, registration fees or exhibit rentals, as well as from public subscriptions. Often the church or city inviting the convention agrees to raise the necessary funds. Advertising space in programs is some-times sold.

INVITATION (ATTENDANCE)

The invitation (attendance) committee will see that the constituency receives the proper invitation to the convention. This duty requires more than the mere issuing of announce-ments. Real sales ability is needed. A strong program may have been arranged, the transportation committee may be ready and the budget may be financed, but these items will not guarantee a full delegation. Infinite patience and fol-low-up are required to produce the results desired. This is especially true of religious organizations, delegates of which must pay their own expenses.

LOCAL COMMITTEE ON ARRANGEMENTS

While the work of the local committee on arrangements covers in time a much shorter period than does that of some of the other committees, the organization is more complex. Under the supervision of this committee will come almost all the subcommittees.

SUBCOMMITTEES

Reception. Nothing counts more than first impressions. The work of the reception committee is therefore most important. Who has not felt the loneliness of coming to a strange church or city without a welcome? To be met at the train, taken to the convention hall for registration, and made to feel at home puts one in a pleasant frame of mind. And if every delegate is cheerful and eager at the first sessions, the convention is well on its way to success.

Registration. It is important to register each delegate as soon as he arrives. This provides a check on the expected attendance, aids in items of publicity, and is of general assistance in all the plans for the entertainment of the guests. A card record is helpful in this department. At the time of registration, fees are collected, assignment to the entertainment committee is made, and each delegate is usually handed an envelope containing his supplies, such as badge, program, notebook, songbook, instructions, etc.

Entertainment. The entertainment committee, having learned in advance of the anticipated attendance, and having been informed especially as to the distinguished speakers and guests who are expected, will secure the necessary reservations in hotels or homes and, possibly with the aid of such organizations as the Boy Scouts, will see that the delegates are taken to their various places of assignment, and shown such other courtesies as the occasion may demand. The entertainment committee may arrange also for luncheons or suppers in or near the convention building and provide special sightseeing tours, concerts, and other features of recreation as may be announced in the program. It is often possible to give an educational pageant or music festival, a pleasant and inspiring way of covering at least part of the expenses of the convention.

Ushers. The ushers' committee may accomplish for a convention what ushers do for a church or theater. The usher's welcome may have marked effect in contributing to the atmosphere of the meetings we attend. Ushers should be carefully instructed as to seating, exits, ventilation, and all emergencies such as sudden illness or accident, possible fire, etc.

Music. To this committee may be assigned the duties of securing leaders of congregational singing, as well as organists or pianists; the furnishing of songbooks, if needed; and the selection of soloists, orchestras, bands, quartets or chorus choirs.

Publicity. This is an important committee, and will function before and after as well as during the convention. There are a great many mediums of publicity which may be used — cards, tickets, circular letters, bulletins, posters, broadcasting and the religious and secular press, for example. Newspaper editors should be invited to the convention sessions, and should be furnished with advance copies of the official program, addresses, facts, pictures and such other information and material as may be requested. Photographs of the principal officers and speakers are usually desired. It is well to arrange also for a picture of the entire delegation.

Recreation. Only those who have attended long, drawn-out convention sessions or conferences lasting far into the night can appreciate the refreshment of variety which may be afforded by careful planning by the recreation committee. Sometimes the program may include sightseeing; at other times, competitive sports or social events. Local conditions will determine what is best. This committee will cooperate closely with the entertainment committee.

Pulpit Supply. If the convention is religious, and holds over Sunday, great benefit may come from an arrangement for the supply of pulpits by the convention speakers and delegates. Sometimes a minister and a layman will go to church together, and both will take part in the service. This puts the community in touch with the purposes of the convention, gives the regular ministers a rest, and is helpful, as well, to those who participate.

Information. What can compare with the usefulness of a good information bureau? A pleasant greeting and a question answered not only aids but cheers the delegate. The information bureau will furnish programs, timetables, directories, maps, stationery and postage, telegraph service, telephones, circulars, bulletins and booklets, and all such information or means to secure it as may be needed. " Courtesy " should be the key word of this committee.

Banquet. Almost every convention schedules a banquet. In business conventions the banquet generally comes last because it is one of the most attractive features of entertainment and helps to hold the delegates to the end of the sessions. Tickets may be prepared in advance and may be sold or given out by the banquet committee, that should know just how many will attend and prepare for them accordingly.

A good menu is essential. There should be a speakers' table, preferably raised a little higher than the others, with place cards indicating the order of seating.

If suitable for the occasion, music is helpful, especially

that which unites the guests in cheerful or devotional singing. A piano should be near the speakers' table. Other music is pleasant if it does not annoy the guests who are con-
versing.

The program for the banquet will depend somewhat upon
the time allowed and the nature of the convention. It should
be positive, but not heavy. It should sum up what has gone
before and should send the guests away in a happy frame of
mind.

A good toastmaster will know not only how to introduce
the speakers, but how and when to call out unexpected
talent from the guests assembled. It is always desirable to
call on newly elected officers, and to express appreciation to
those who may be chiefly responsible for the success of the
meeting.

Flowers will form the chief decoration, especially for the
speakers' table. Flags and bunting are sometimes appropriate.

The gathering together of a group of delegates in any
well managed convention will accomplish more in a day
than could be achieved in months, if not years, of effort on
the part of individuals acting independently.

A large proportion of America's business is conducted on
the basis of personal friendship. Many of the most important transactions take place over the dinner table or on the
golf course at the country club. How much more important
it is, then, that through the fellowship afforded by good conventions, ministers and others engaged in Christian service
may come to know one another personally for the promotion
of " the biggest business in the world " on a basis of mutual
confidence and good will.

CHAPTER THIRTEEN

THE SWINDLING OF MINISTERS

THAT ministers are an easy prey for professional beggars and crooks is well known, but that there is alleged to exist a nation-wide clearinghouse of information available to those who make it a business to relieve these worthy gentlemen of their hard-earned cash will doubtless be a surprise to many.

A stranger calls to see the minister, brings greetings from one of the deacons of his previous church, volunteers items of personal information, and expresses his appreciation of the sermon preached by the minister on a recent visit to a neighboring town. The minister does not remember meeting the man, but the circumstances are all so familiar that he takes him into his confidence. " By the way," says the stranger, " I find that I have not brought enough money with me to get back home. Can you cash a small check? " Where did this stranger secure his information, and what shall the minister do?

According to one of the leading ministers of America, who admits that he has been duped several times by the " clever boys," " the evidence is conclusive that there exists a clearinghouse or bureau for the purpose of furnishing these details at so much a case. Conventions of ministers are studied, names and details are given, and the swindlers are furnished the information desired from these resources."

The swindling of ministers has been taking place systematically all over the country, though most of it is confined to the areas of the larger cities. Rural sections are visited by tramps for whom meals and lodging are the price generally paid by the minister. " These tramps behave pretty well," says one minister in central Illinois, " because our telephones work fast, and it does not take long to inform the neighbors along the way."

WHAT A SURVEY SHOWS

The situation has become so alarming in the cities that in answer to the appeals from many of its alumni, the Chicago Theological Seminary, through its department of business administration, conducted a nation-wide survey to determine the extent of the work of these professional crooks, and to ascertain whether or not such thefts could be prevented in the future by warnings to those now in service, and by proper instruction to young ministers in training in theological seminaries. Questionnaires were sent out and conferences were held asking for the experiences of men in various communities in dealing with actual situations. Among the questions asked were: " Do you believe in punishing such crooks? " and " How may they be detected as being different from worthy cases of need? "

The response was so generous that a number of definite conclusions were reached which ought to be of help to ministers everywhere.

The amounts of money lost, individually, were comparatively small, ranging mostly from one dollar to ten dollars, but reaching occasionally from fifty to one hundred dollars. The greater calamity to the minister is his loss of faith in human nature.

"Jesus did not distinguish between the crook and the worthy man when he suggested that we should give to those who ask of us," wrote one minister. "He was probably thinking as much of the effect of the gift upon the giver as upon the man who asked it. To refuse to help even the unworthy means that we have in so far hardened our hearts. Nor are crooks remade by detention and punishment or through being sent away empty, but by lavish giving, as in the case of Jean Valjean."

TYPES OF SWINDLE

The methods of swindling ministers may be divided into three general groups:

(1) *The "temporary loan" or the cashing of checks.* This appeal is based generally on stereotyped appeals, as pocketbook lost or stolen, mother dying in nearby town, and, has been out of work, but now has position in another place, and needs only transportation to get there.

(2) *The local business swindle.* Here payments are made in advance on supposed bona fide contracts, such as fake church directories, magazine and book subscriptions, and worthless correspondence courses.

(3) *The purchase of worthless securities.* These are sold, for investment purposes, as ownership in stocks and bonds, oil wells and refineries, mining properties, pecan or lemon groves in Florida or California, real-estate subdivisions in unknown places, silver fox ranches, rabbit and chicken farms and inexpensive insurance.

Many ministers are swindled by professional crooks because of their interpretations of such biblical passages as: "If any man . . . take away thy coat, let him have thy cloak also" (Matt. 5:40). "Pray for them which despite-fully use you" (Matt. 5:44). "For I was an hungred, and ye gave me meat: I was thirsty, and ye gave me drink: I was a stranger, and ye took me in: Naked, and ye clothed me: I was sick, and ye visited me: I was in prison, and ye came unto me" (Matt. 25:35–36). "Inasmuch as ye did it not to one of the least of these, ye did it not to me" (Matt. 25:45).

"What did Jesus mean," they ask in all sincerity, "when he said in the Sermon on the Mount, 'Give to him that asketh thee, and from him that would borrow of thee, turn thou not away'?" (Matt. 5:42).

"I would rather be swindled a dozen times," is the common testimony of ministers, "than to turn away one deserving case."

Ministers are on the so-called "sucker-list," according to one authority, because they lack business experience, they are moved by sentiment and yield to high-powered sales talks, and their training for the ministry has taught them to have faith in human nature just as they find it, in every station and condition of life.

MINISTERS' WIVES AS VICTIMS

"The crooks even make a business of circularizing a minister's wife," according to a Wisconsin pastor. "For several years my wife had letters from oil companies all over the South, saying that they knew that ministers' wives often felt the need of a little money of their own, and offering large returns on small investments. After receiving dozens of such letters, my wife finally wrote to them, asking if they were not ashamed to try to coax the small savings from poor ministers' wives, who always needed their money? The strange thing about it was that, while the letters had been coming from different companies from several states, this one letter stopped them all."

One of the reasons why ministers are easy marks is that usually they may be found alone in their homes or offices, whereas the businessman is somewhat protected by his private secretary and business associates. In office buildings, the telephone is handy and policemen are near, whereas the minister very rarely makes application to the law.

It is almost universal testimony that theological seminaries have not given practical training for dealing with problems of this kind. "I thank you for putting me on my guard," wrote a minister in Vermont. "You may add my name to the list of those who have been swindled," stated another in California, "for I was buncoed this noon, with your letter of warning lying open on my desk." "I think a chair ought to be established in every seminary," testified a minister in Florida, "to teach the students the difference between a man of vision and a visionary man; between day-dreaming and common-sense thinking; between real investments and gambling; and a host of other similar subjects over which ministers stumble and fall."

SOME EXAMPLES

"I am trying to keep from growing hard-boiled," says a minister in California, "for I am writing this letter on a secondhand typewriter instead of my good one, which was stolen recently. I might have prevented that theft by being more suspicious. The thief heard me using the machine in the office, and lured me outside to say that he was moving near us, with his mother, and had a rug which would not fit their new home. He wanted to know if they might place it in the church. He would be ready soon to transfer his membership to us. I checked as many facts as I could, but the next morning my typewriter was gone, and so was the man. Three nights ago my church office was smashed in by heavy timbers," he continued. " Any coins for telephone, missions, birthday, etc. are bait for burglars. I expect three or four such robberies every year. Train our young ministers to be wise as serpents."

" I was in bed with the smallpox," testified a minister in Montana. " A foreigner came to the door and asked for a small loan. He said he had just moved to a little town twenty miles away. He needed money for a shipment of plants to start business. He gave me the name of his minister. All facts corresponded with information in the Year Book. I advanced him the funds, which he promised to return within a week. He never came back. I wrote to the minister; he had never heard of the name."

" The fellow with a ready-made story and a glib mouth is invariably the one to watch," wrote a minister in Kansas. " About three keen questions checking back on some former statement will usually trip him. A minister should not be hard-boiled, but sometimes he needs to be hard-headed."

Here is another point of view, from a minister in Wyoming, who says: " I have never been swindled by any man. Always we have believed that whoever came to our door was sent to us by the Father of Love. A tramp, so called, comes to the door, and is admitted as a brother. He is fed with food both for his body and for his soul, and with the sympathy given, we usually think he tells the truth. If a swindler entered our home, he would soon know that we were thinking so well of him that he would reveal his best to us. There is no fear in love."

"I recall a man who came to prayer meeting," wrote a Pennsylvania clergyman. "He made a good 'testimony' and was lavish in his praise of my address. The next day he called on me and told me he was a missionary of a small sect; he was expecting a remittance at the next station, and asked if I would advance him the price of a ticket. I 'advanced' and he blessed me and departed. That was long ago, but I have not received his remittance. I heard afterward that he had fleeced others. His gushing piousness should have put me on my guard."

"They commonly wear the mask of religion," said a Denver pastor with fifteen years of experience. "They come with a pitiful story of need. They tell of relatives to whom they have already sent for money, and it requires but a few days to procure it. Meanwhile, they seek my assistance to sustain them until their money shall come, with the promise always that it shall be returned. Frequently they come to me after worship on Sunday mornings, when the banks and the post office are closed. I know of no way for a preacher to guard himself against these people. If he meets their wishes he is considered soft; and these fellows seem to have ways of conveying this knowledge to others. If he turns them down both he and his church get the reputation of being unchristian, and the minister then carries the thought that possibly he may have denied a worthy case. And so the ministers continue to be victimized.

"A man will appear in my office, and will have sufficient acquaintance with brother ministers in other parts of the country to convince the most unbelieving. I had one man call and tell me that his little girl had just died, and that he needed ten dollars with which to procure some necessary items for her burial. I gave him the ten dollars, arranged with an undertaker to bury his child without cost, and sent the undertaker to the address which he gave, and behold, no such address was to be found in the city."

" I lost my savings in mining stock," wrote a prominent leader in North Dakota. " Later, I lived in Colorado, and was surprised to find that for every mine in that state, where there was any reasonable prospect of success, money could be raised in Denver to finance it on twenty-four hours' notice."

" It seems too bad that a minister of Christ should need to be on the defensive toward his fellow men, especially those who come seeking help and protection," testified a minister in Texas. " Yet most of us learn sooner or later, by experience, to erect a guard about ourselves against imposters and swindlers who prey upon those whose calling exposes them to all sorts of appeals. I learned this very early in my ministry, when a crook, a clever religious pretender, not only robbed me of my clothing and other personal belongings, but actually assumed my name and title in another city, and for several months played the role of a popular preacher in a denominational pulpit until exposed by an uncommon ability to write forged checks."

Here is counsel from a minister in Illinois, who admits that he has been helping crooks all his life: " Sometimes they were stragglers who wandered in from nowhere, and often they were in the pews more or less regularly. One was a church trustee whose reputation was made known to me by outside friends, and yet the church would not look up the man or accept any evidence until a good number had been swindled. Most of us ministers must face such people often, and yet we are expected to be pious and to give these men a new chance, as if that were what was wanted. Recently a man and woman worked an advertising scheme on us, pretending to get up a church directory. They pocketed the money collected, but did not deliver the advertising. My counsel is to give no help to outside parties without looking up the facts. The average police and local officers, as a rule, are much saner, and possess just as great a desire to help these people, only the minister does not think so; and therefore he must learn by experience."

It is almost universal testimony that money loaned to strangers is never paid back. It is better to count such loans as gifts, and never to depend upon their repayment. " They write down my name and address, and promise to send the money back within a week, but the week turns to years and the money is never returned. Nobody has ever returned my money; I must have turned down the deserving and helped the crooks."

" What counsel would you give young ministers? " was asked of the head of the Christian Industrial League in Chicago. " I would make it hard for the stranger to get money," was the reply. Ministers are bothered by undeserving men because it is easy to get their help. If there could be a united policy among the ministers, their troubles would straighten out themselves.

" I have paid bonuses to many liars for deceiving me with plausible stories," declares a minister of a night church in a large city, " and yet I have never prosecuted any of those who victimized me." The very nature of his work prevents a minister from seeking justice, and yet how easy it makes it for the crooks to proceed with their schemes.

INVESTIGATE FIRST

Another type of swindling is represented by the man who would present an unknown cause to the congregation of the church. " A very plausible appeal was made to me recently," wrote an Iowa clergyman, " by a man, evidently from the Near East, who was collecting funds for the ancient churches of Mosul. He had letters of recommendation from at least twenty-five of the neighboring ministers. I told him that I would wire to the state office and elsewhere to verify his story, and that I would let him know in the morning what I would do. By morning he had left town, getting a man to drive him, at a most unreasonable hour, to a neighboring town for his train. The only safe policy is to do nothing for such pleaders until the proper information has been secured."

" It is not unchristian to investigate the propositions presented to us by strangers," according to an Ohio pastor, " or to be hard-boiled in listening to a lot of sob-sister appeals. Some of these crooks begin by flattering us; they have just come in from the old home town, and they tell us what fine things they have heard about us. They purr over us like old tabby cats. Do I believe in punishing such crooks? Why not? Is a professional crook more entitled to consideration than any other criminal? But the question which the church and the minister must face is deeper than that: What leads a man to be a professional crook? What are we doing in our churches to prevent our boys and our girls from becoming moral derelicts? What effect has it upon them to see a professional crook get away with his deviltry? This whole question has its constructive, common-sense phase, and its wishy-washy side. The bastille for the adult professional crook! How may they be detected from worthy cases of need? It takes knowledge and experience, and there is a sympathetic side to these matters, but we cannot trifle with flagrant dishonesty."

"Once when I lived in a mountain town," testified a minister in Omaha, "a man came to me asking for the price of a pair of shoes. His bare toes were sticking out. He was wet to the skin from head to foot. He said he had walked over the mountains twenty-four miles. He looked the part. I sent him to a shoe store and telephoned the merchant in advance to give him two pairs of warm socks and a strong pair of shoes; to let him choose what he wanted, and to charge them to me. He put on the new shoes and had the old ones wrapped up. Two hours later, as I was going home, I saw the fellow on the street again, drunk, and wearing his old shoes. I am convinced by long experience and from contact with charity workers that almost all who come to our doors as strangers, or who beg on the streets, are professionals."

Women, as well as men, are found among the swindlers. "One day when we were living in a small town in South Dakota," wrote one pastor, "a woman plainly but comfortably dressed came to our door. She had a pathetic story to tell, of having been robbed of her pocketbook while she was asleep on the train. When a new conductor came on, she had no ticket and no money; so he put her off at our station. She asked if I would lend her enough money to get to the next town, where she had a job waiting for her, as cook in a hotel. From her conversation, she seemed to be an earnest Christian. We bought her a ticket and put her on the train. With a warm good-bye, and with many blessings called down from heaven, she thanked us for our kindness, and promised that as soon as she secured her first wages she would return the loan; but evidently she has never had her wages, for the money has not been received. If anything can be done to protect ministers and their wives from yielding to such appeals you will be doing a good deed."

PROTECTIVE MEASURES

And now as to the conclusions: " Beware of the man with the sick mother-in-law whom he wants to see before she dies," warns one clergyman, " for that game is as old as grandmother's funeral on a baseball day." A Cleveland pastor said that in the twenty-six years of his ministry, he has yet to see the first honest case of a man asking for money.

" I would like to suggest," wrote an Ohio minister who has had fifteen years' experience in dealing with the down-and-outers, " that the main object should be to discover and remedy the cause of the trouble, rather than just to deal with the symptoms. Therefore:

(1) " No ordinary minister should rely wholly upon his own judgment in handling such cases. They should be turned over to the proper organizations, the welfare societies, manned by experts, with adequate machinery for investigation and assistance. (Should there not be such an organization, it might be more worth while to turn one's efforts toward the forming of such a board than to try to solve such questions alone.)

(2) " No minister should give money to such persons.

Give food, if needed, by taking the solicitor to a restaurant and paying for the meal; give friendly counsel, without condescension. The Scriptural injunction, 'Give to him that asketh,' can only be fulfilled by giving oneself to see that the proper organizations, including the churches, do this work thoroughly, and promptly and kindly.

(3) "Organize and support your organization, and see that it does its work. This will probably take more time and energy than doing the work alone."

"Apply the work test," wrote an Indiana minister of mature experience. "Most of the crooks will not respond to a demand for work in return for assistance given.

"Build a reputation for investigating. A reputation can be made that will keep away a great many undeserving cases.

"Study people, particularly their eyes and their feet. A man that is telling a lie may be able to look you in the eye, and may be able to manage his hands, but he will tend to exhibit nervousness in shuffling his feet."

"Never lend money to a stranger," counseled a Georgia pastor. "The banks have money for that purpose. If the stranger's credit is good, the banks will accept it; if not, it is no good to me. And never give a letter of recommendation to a stranger. The crook business is getting so bad that there is a service that someone should render to the ministry. When I was secretary of a Kiwanis Club, I noted that the international secretary required that we report each month concerning any crooks that descended upon our club. This list was published and sent to every one of the thirteen hundred clubs. Every secretary was on the watch to detect any such intrusion and avoid further trouble. Could not some such plan be worked out for the church? By a united effort to defeat it, this business of swindling the ministers would soon prove to be unprofitable."

A Chicago minister of many years' experience gave this advice: " A telephone message reports that a tubercular patient is stranded in Chicago and needs immediate aid for the purchase of a railroad ticket to go west. Later, the person calls, mentions the names of well known denominational leaders, and shows copies of telegrams from them. Give no money. Consult the Chicago Tubercular Society and the Travelers' Aid, as well as the United Charities."

Or, " An alleged young intern has just arrived in Chicago from the West; he has a position with one of the hospitals, but he must purchase his uniform, costing eight dollars, before he can go to work. He will repay out of his first month's salary. Call the hospital mentioned, while he is there, and see what happens."

" We have a pastor's fund and a church fund for the cases of need in our own community," wrote a Pittsburgh minister, " but as for the constant stream of floaters who live on the work of others, we tell them frankly we have none to give; if they desire food or raiment, we refer them to the Associated Charities or others of the many welfare organizations supported by the community."

" In the larger cities where organized social work is established, such a reference on the part of the clergymen would preclude all but the rarest cases of swindling," said a Chicago minister.

" Concerning the purchase of worthless securities," testified an Illinois minister who was recently swindled out of all his life savings, " in financial matters, trust no man. Before paying for any security, examine its source. The county recorder will tell you all about any piece of land. I made the mistake of not asking him. I trusted a man, and he ruined me. Tell the young ministers these things, for I was once young and would have appreciated such advice."

" I think if a man would be careful to investigate before he gave help, most of these problems would be solved," said one of Detroit's leading preachers. " It is always best to send a telegram to the city from which the man says he came, and to insist upon making a personal investigation before doing anything. The crooks have a habit of ' fading away ' when one uses this method. Of course, a man does not cease to be a man, even if he is a crook, and there may be a chance to be of service to him."

ADVICE OF SOCIAL AGENCIES

As an example of methods to pursue, I present here the advice of Chicago social agencies to ministers around that city. Other cities might follow suit.

The Chicago Council of Social Agencies offered this counsel, through its director: " I am of the opinion that ministers having no trained social service facilities in connection with their church organizations, through which cases of this type might be considered, could well adopt a rather rigid policy of referring such appeals to organizations equipped to determine the validity of requests and to serve their needs. These requests are of two general types: The first is the individual who begs your sympathy by means of a distressing story; and the second is the representative who presents himself as attached to some organized charitable or philanthropic service.

" In the case of the first type, it is a safe plan for the minister to refer the individual to the proper organization. With regard to appeals from persons claiming to represent philanthropic and charitable organizations, it would be well to advise all ministers to confer with the Subscriptions Investigating Committee of the Chicago Association of Commerce. All qualified charitable organizations in Chicago are endorsed by this committee. The minister might also confer with the Chicago Council of Social Agencies which has information about qualified and unqualified charitable organizations in Chicago."

According to the United Charities of Chicago, " the handling of strangers who come to the offices of ministers is a social service responsibility.

" If these men or women say that they are residents of Chicago, or if they say that they have families living elsewhere, it seems to me that it would be best to send them to the nearest district office of the United Charities. If men are single and homeless, I think it would be wise to send them to one of the organizations that are equipped to deal with that type of individual, for example, the Christian Industrial League, the Goodwill Industries of Chicago, the Salvation Army, the Cathedral Shelter, the Municipal Lodging House, etc.

" If the minister who has the original interview will telephone to the place to which he is sending the man, an appointment can be arranged. The United Charities will be glad to report to the minister concerning the case, and without doubt all other social agencies would do the same.

" If a minister wishes to do so, he can get a book of tickets from the Christian Industrial League. Each ticket provides the applicant with a bed for the night and breakfast in the morning. It is not necessary to pay for these tickets unless they are used."

" I used this plan for more than a year," wrote a prominent minister in Boston. " I would give the applicant one of these tickets saying: ' This will entitle you to a supper and a clean bed, regardless of your circumstances. In the morning, you will have the opportunity of talking to the superintendent, who will help you to find work and a permanent means of support. At any hour, you will find a person in charge at the address given on the ticket. The cost of your supper and lodging will be charged to me by the bureau, and I will pay it.'

" These tickets cost me twenty-five cents each, and in the course of a year I gave away seventy-five or eighty of them. I have sometimes asked friends to guess how much it cost me to be so generous. The bill was staggering — fifty cents! Out of all those applicants, only two cared enough for what they sought to present the tickets."

" During my three years in a prominent church in St. Louis," testified another clergyman, who received frequent appeals for help, " I discovered just one man who I believe was honest. He was an Irishman who had studied for the priesthood at Notre Dame University, and had been expelled for drunkenness. He said, ' Father, all I want is a quarter for a flop, and I have no time to argue. If you won't give it to me, I'll simply go to the next party, and continue until I get it.' "

In all the testimony received from twenty-four states, only one minister recommended punishment for crooks and swindlers. Throughout the investigation, a spirit of interest and sympathy was evident. There appeared to be little regret over financial losses sustained. A desire seemed everywhere prevalent that worthy cases may be recognized and helped. All that was asked in return, was that ministers might be protected from further inroads on their meager incomes by unworthy crooks and swindlers.

Chapter Fourteen

EXECUTIVE LEADERSHIP

THE LADDER of life's leadership is crowded at the bottom but almost empty at the top.

A certain church in a college town lost its pastor. The salary offered was twenty-five hundred dollars. Within six months, the pulpit committee had received four hundred applications from other ministers.

The church that can pay from five thousand to seventy-five hundred dollars for its preaching must look far and wide for a leader, and often he is taken from another denomination.

When a salary of ten thousand dollars or more is offered, it is almost impossible to find the right man. Why? Because the church requires of him the proper balance as preacher, pastor and business administrator, and comparatively few men in the Christian ministry are ready for the call.

The executive of a large church must carry responsibilities as important as are those of the manager of a business enterprise. In the first place, he must know men. He must be familiar with the forces which move men to action and which keep them loyal to the tasks at hand. He must understand the principles of organization with the minimum of supervision for groups both paid and volunteer.

He may find himself in charge of properties in which from five hundred thousand to a million dollars has been invested.

Or perhaps he is called upon to construct new buildings. He must have at least a sense of good architecture. He comes at once into the problems of plans and specifications, acoustics, color schemes, bids, contracts, insurance, bonds, mortgages and campaigns of finance.

He must understand engineering because there are furnaces, boilers, elevators, machinery and electrical equipment the proper care of which is vitally important to the services of his church.

THE MINISTER'S ACTIVITIES

He must be an educator, for his church school reaches much farther than does the work of the public school, taking a life, as it does, " from the cradle to the grave."

He will be the manager of a club, for the social activities of his church will require an intimate knowledge of the psychology of entertainment.

The minister of a large church must be a businessman, for his annual budget will run from twenty-five to one hundred thousand dollars and this amount must not only be raised, but its expenditure must be carefully supervised and checked. He must understand reports, and he will study their trends to catch weaknesses.

The successful minister must be a physician, for many of the problems that come to him will be traced easily to mental and physical illness.

He may rightly be named a " trouble adjuster," for he will be called upon to conduct an employment bureau. He may need to dispense food and supplies to the poor, and he must understand the technique of organized charity.

He must be a statesman, whose knowledge and interest

will include not only local civic affairs, but those of state, national and world-wide scope. As a Christian diplomat, his influence and his programs of service will reach out to his entire denomination, and beyond that he will inform himself concerning the interdenominational movements, from his own community to those of international breadth, and he will take part in their promotion.

He must be a parliamentarian, for he will be called upon to conduct large and important assemblies.

The executive-minister will be an editor and publisher, familiar with styles of type, proof reading and press work, for the program of the church requires bulletins, leaflets, booklets and magazines.

He must be familiar with advertising and publicity, for his membership of from one to two thousand is a force in the community which should be publicly recognized, and which should reach out to ever enlarging circles of influence.

He will be a traveler, with an intimate knowledge of hotels, trains, steamships and airplanes at home and abroad. He may find it convenient and useful to master two or three foreign languages for purposes of conversation, reading and correspondence.

He must understand the catering business, for many meals will be served in his church, ranging from afternoon teas to banquets for a thousand people.

Who would think of the minister as a showman? And yet drama, lighting and other stage effects must be well known to him, for these are required in the program of the modern church.

As priest, he will lead great services of worship. As prophet, he will be keen of vision, for he must see ahead and deal with controversial subjects. As missionary, he will represent all the interests of the Christian church.

He must be a man among men; a creator of good will; a student of all that concerns the lives of his congregation.

And all of these things he must do, not with authority, but by persuasion. His patience must be unlimited, his courage indomitable, and his wisdom infinite. He must devise new ways to make old programs interesting, remembering that people become tired of repetition.

When he has become expert in all of these duties, and many more, he will be a super-executive, and there are churches that are waiting for his leadership, where the item of salary is no object either to him or to the congregations which desire his services.

I have often wondered why so many ministers limit their opportunities for success by a seeming unwillingness to consider the administrative and promotional side of their work.

Times have changed since men were called only to preach.

It is the duty of ministers to put men to work for the church, in order that they may grow in grace and wisdom, and that through their training, their interests may extend to new channels of service in their daily living, until all the needs of a Christian community are met in full.

THE BUSINESS OPPORTUNITY

I wonder if the younger ministers realize how great a business opportunity is placed before them. A layman, for example, may work faithfully for years, and yet he may never reach the top of his profession; but a minister, even one just graduated from seminary, is placed at the head of a ready-made organization, with the assumption in advance that should it become necessary or desirable for him to move to another community, whether successful or not in his present field, his position of leadership will be renewed, and he will continue as the director of a promising, if not of a thriving church business. What, then, will he do with his opportunity?

It is said that the presence of Napoleon on the field of battle was equal in value to forty thousand men. How many men is a minister worth as an executive, in the daily conquests of his church?

There are three points involved in executive leadership: A goal to reach; a force to direct; the ability and the training to organize and direct the forces to reach the goal.

NOT BY AUTHORITY

The great difference between a military, political or business executive and the minister is that in religious work there is no authority without the individual and collective consent of the governed. The business executive may require obedience; the minister cannot.

In many cases, the minister meets strong wills differing from his own. How shall he put them to work for the church? He may find cowardice or selfishness or indifference or desire for the limelight and publicity. All of these problems he must meet.

In almost any congregation the minister will discover those who know more than he does about certain phases of the program. How shall he weld these forces into an organization which will recognize him as their administrative head? His task is so unlike that of the business administrator that it is seldom understood by the layman. It is one of the reasons why so-called " business efficiency " alone will not make a church successful.

If the minister is to be a leader, he must provide a worthy program working toward definite goals before he can enlist or organize the forces at his command. The majority of church activities are too narrow in their outlook to interest their constituencies. They include plenty of work for the ministers, but little for the members of the congregations.

LAY LEADERSHIP

The second item in the minister's executive work involves the forces that he is to direct. With rare exceptions, there is as much hidden or undeveloped talent in any church group as is needed for the program of that group. Often I have heard ministers say, " We have no leadership in our church." I wonder why.

I once attended a book publishers' convention, where the subject presented was " How to Pick Good Salesmen." This, of course, is one of the most important questions in any business organization. The methods outlined by an enthusiastic young sales manager were so conclusive that from a group of men and women standing before us we could select the promising salespeople almost without error. About the time we reached this conclusion, one of the older and more successful publishers arose and said, " Gentlemen, out of these one hundred prospects, you may pick your fifty best salesmen, and I shall take the fifty who remain, and I shall train them, and we shall sell as many books as your fifty." And he was right. Why? Because every one of the second fifty would have parents, brothers, sisters, friends and acquaintances — a clientele which could be reached successfully if the salesman were properly trained. And so it is with the church. Jesus might have selected his disciples from the leaders of his time, but he chose to turn to the more humble souls who had " listening hearts," and to these he gave his time and attention, until they were ready to lay down their lives for his cause.

The third requirement of executive leadership concerns the minister's direction and organization of the forces to reach the goal. It is the minister's duty to multiply himself. Except in the case of the larger churches, practically all help must be voluntary. Certain leaders will be found in every group who seem especially interested and efficient in their work. These should be commended, encouraged and promoted. Whenever a helper comes with a suggestion let him work it out if it is feasible. One by one, the minister will win these friends to his active staff. Others will need to be discovered. He must find them and patiently train them for their tasks.

Sometimes it is necessary to replace seemingly inefficient helpers, and this is not always easily accomplished. If it is not done in the right way and in the right spirit, friction is likely to result. In such cases, it may be best to transfer or to promote the workers to other positions, just as a business house might do, even though it may be necessary to create new offices to fit the peculiar talents of the persons involved.

HOW NOT TO DO IT

One of the saddest failures I have ever known in this connection is a fine young minister who was called to a church where there had been considerable friction in previous pastorates. He reached the conclusion after a few weeks that the only way to straighten out the difficulties was to get rid of at least ten of the trouble-makers in the congregation. It took him two years to remove these people from the church, and within two months of that time he was out of the church himself. Why? Because the ten members dismissed had friends among those who were left, and reaction set in against him. Soon afterward he left the ministry, so great was his disappointment and suffering. Meantime, the chairman of his board, a banker, had come to me and said, " We want to raise our pastor's salary, and everything is all set to do it if he would only stop rubbing the fur the wrong way with so many of our people."

Ministers who are great preachers are likely to attract large followings to themselves. They may even instill the desire for service, but may not have the ability to put men to work. Such leaders need either paid or volunteer helpers or assistants who will supplement their drawing powers with the talents of organization and administration. Unfortunately, some preachers do not know how to use the services of paid assistants, strange as this may seem. They do not know how to " let go," to trust others. It seems easier for them to do the work themselves. This is brought out in the following letter from a prominent pastor in New York:

" In one of our conferences recently, one of our strongest men was forced to resign from a promising church because he insisted on doing all the work himself and did not know how to use a secretary or an assistant. The church agreed to hire both.

" Though a college- and seminary-trained man, he was

forced to admit his inability to employ the help that was offered. As a result, he has had to take a small church, and his usefulness has thereby suffered to a very large extent."

The minister's task is to create constructive and profitable work for others, and not for himself.

When work is well done, its worth should be recognized, if possible, publicly. Sometimes just a little pen-written note from one's pastor is a sufficient reward.

CHECKING UP

Many battles in life are lost for the lack of what is termed the " follow-up." The business executive knows from the reports on his desk whether or not his assignments have had attention. The minister must find out in other ways; perhaps by conferences, personal calls or reports at meetings. It matters not so much how or where the check takes place, but human nature is such that there must be a follow-up if the work is to progress successfully.

Multitudes of assignments have died a natural death for lack of follow-up, and efficient workers have been lost for the church. One might as well plant a garden and then go off and forget about it.

In former days it was the custom for the leader of an army to fight at the head of his troops. His influence was somewhat dependent upon his personal valor. Now he stays at the rear of the conflict and sends out the younger men to battle. There is a lesson here for us. Many a minister, in a spirit of impatience at the lack of progress, has forged ahead with his plans in advance of his constituency. History is filled with the tragedies of enthusiastic leaders who have fallen by the wayside because they could not wait. It is better to remain in the background until the plans are ready and the organization is perfected to perform the tasks at hand.

The minister who promotes his program by high-pressure methods is sure to suffer a sad reaction. Suppose, for instance, he forces the adoption of a new budget or of a building program before his trustees are convinced that it is best for the church. Is he not likely later to find himself facing the necessity of raising the money with opposition instead of support?

Every new movement should seem to originate with the committee or constituency directly responsible. I know of a minister who secured the funds to install a pipe organ which was greatly needed in his church, but his efforts were never appreciated because the subject had not been passed upon by the music committee or been considered favorably by the congregation.

How, then, is a minister to promote the advance steps of his program? By conferring first with key individuals, according to the interests or officials involved; then with groups, committees, departments; and perhaps finally, if needed, with their backing and approval, by presenting the project to the entire congregation. Thus through tactfulness and methods of education it has become at last not his, but their united program.

No minister who likes to show his authority can be a true executive, for " every display of authority lessens authority." He governs best who seems to govern the least. The authority of a real leader will be felt rather than seen.

NEVER THREATEN TO RESIGN

Sometimes ministers are guilty of forcing situations by threatening to resign. There came to my attention recently the case of a young minister who was greatly beloved by his church, so much so that they gave him a beautiful home and were intending, in time, to build a new church. But he became restless. He wanted the church built sooner than was planned; in fact, he became so troubled over the situation that he threatened to resign, and was ready to accept the call to another church unless his parishioners went ahead.

It was a difficult situation to face, both for the minister and for the church. It was not good salesmanship. The minister won; but in doing so he also lost, for neither he nor his church was happy about it, and the former relations of friendship and trust could not continue. It was not long before he left the church and accepted another pastorate.

Every executive should conserve his physical resources. It is the surplus of energy — the enthusiastic overflow of life — that makes him stand out as a leader. He must be creative. If a minister wastes his time on details that should be assigned to others, or pours out his strength on needless tasks, his power will be undermined.

It seems to me that the minister-executive, above all men, should cultivate a pleasing personality. He must like people and bring out the best that is in them. Personality is to a man what perfume is to a flower. It is not the flower itself, but that delicate fragrance which it breathes out to others. It wins the faith and love of little children. It comforts the sorrowing. It inspires confidence and wholesomeness and loyalty in one's associates.

The pastor of a church should be a man of poise; without it he cannot hope to lead. When all about him may seem in confusion, his quietness and self-control will still the tempest. There is a certain strength about people with poise that makes others desire to follow them. They are like the solid rock which cannot be washed away in time of storm.

COST OF LEADERSHIP

There is a cost, however, to executive leadership — a price so great that many do not care to pay it. The higher one rises on the ladder of success, the more he will find himself lonely and alone. Jesus organized the forces for a world-wide church and trained his associates for its leadership; but how little he was understood, even by those who knew him best. His closest friends went to sleep when he needed them most. "He was a man of sorrows and acquainted with grief."

An executive must be ready to bear the full responsibility for all his decisions and their consequences. He must be a man of courage — open to criticism as well as to praise; ready for opposition and oppression as well as for friendship and support. He has been chosen as the shepherd of his flock. He has dedicated his life to Christian service. It is for him to lead. He must not turn aside until the goals of the church have been reached, and he hears again those comforting words (Matt. 25:21): "Well done, thou good and faithful servant; thou hast been faithful over a few things, I will make thee ruler over many things: enter thou into the joy of thy Lord."

CHAPTER FIFTEEN

A MESSAGE TO LAYMEN

THIS BOOK has been written as a manual for ministers, especially the younger men who may have come but recently from their seminaries.

Some day your pastor is going to share it with you, for he will face church problems of finance, organization, convention management and other business subjects on which he will need your help, and when he does so, I want you to read this chapter, which is not intended for him, but for you, as laymen.

I am thinking especially of the new minister whom you may have called to your church. You have not chosen him carelessly, for he is to be your leader in the spiritual life. He is to teach your children. He is to guide you in time of mental and spiritual distress. He is to be your ambassador, not only in your own community, but at businessmen's clubs, high school commencements, and in all the wider councils of the church. You are always to feel proud of him as your representative.

Your pastoral committee has finished its work. Its members doubtless searched far and wide for just the right man. They considered his character, his habits, his appearance, his training, his age and experience, his personality and even his family. They heard him preach. They weighed his prayers and his spiritual life. They investigated his previous work and his references. Now they have turned him over to you, with their recommendation and approval, to become the minister of your church. A new day of hope and expectation is before you.

What will you do, as laymen, to make his administration a success? In receiving your new minister, you should first remember that there are three distinct divisions of his work:

THE MINISTER AS PREACHER

First. He must be a *preacher.* Protestant churches somehow require that our ministers preach to us. There is not very much that you, as layman, can do to help your minister with this part of his program, except, perhaps, to furnish him a good office or study, containing spacious shelves for his library. Of course, you can provide him with the best books and magazines, and with modern office equipment, which are really his preaching tools; and you should allow him opportunity in his daily schedule to use them.

He has spent four years in college and three years or more in postgraduate work at the seminary, under learned men. His time is valuable. He should be furnished with a sufficient staff, either paid or volunteer, or both, and with all possible labor- and time-saving devices to guarantee his happiness and general efficiency.

You should give your minister opportunities for educational travel; and you must see to it, as your duty, that he is sent at your expense to local, state and national church gatherings, in order that he may think in the largest possible terms, and thus keep you in touch with the broader policies of the church. Such items should be included in the regular budget.

Ministers ought to take more vacations than they do, not for rest but for purposes of education. They need to study missions at home and abroad, to confer with denominational leaders, to attend summer schools and other special conferences, and to visit the art galleries, libraries, universities and cathedrals of Europe in order that they may keep out of mental ruts, and thus remain at the head of world thought and international understanding. How can a minister understand the meaning of the Bible until he has seen the Holy Land? Every contribution to his education is an investment in the leadership of the church.

THE MINISTER AS PASTOR

Second. A minister must be a *pastor* — a shepherd of his flock. A shepherd cannot be successful unless the sheep will follow him. If he gets behind them, and tries to drive them, they will scatter. Therefore, he must lead them, and as the holy Scriptures tell us, " they will follow him, because they know his voice."

This means complete loyalty on your part, as layman. Under no circumstances should you criticize your pastor, either publicly or privately, any more than you would censure the most beloved members of your own family. You have installed him as your minister. By so doing, you have made him a very part of you " for better, or for worse."

No divisions should ever be allowed in the church. When there are differences of opinion, almost always it will be found that they refer to methods rather than to purposes. Methods can be adjusted and compromised. A minister can do his best work for us when peace and harmony prevail.

You can help him by constructive suggestions and information concerning every department of church work — and especially with regard to the conditions, needs and opportunities of our present and prospective church homes. You should welcome him at all times, and should consider him an ex-officio member of every committee of the church, seeking his counsel, and keeping him fully informed with regard to all of your official plans and actions.

You laymen ought to take more interest than you do in the minister's home. Is it comfortable, and convenient to his church and work? Is it equipped for his social responsibilities? Is it attractive and in good repair? Is it worthy of your " Kingdom Ambassador "?

Have you met the minister's wife and children? Do you know their names and the dates of their birthdays? Could you not invite them to go with you sometimes to your places of business and amusement? Are they on your Christmas list?

Nothing is more necessary to a minister in his pastoral work than an automobile. One of the best financial investments that a church can make is to provide its pastor with a good car, or its equivalent in salary or traveling expense allowance. How can you expect your minister to call upon you willingly and quickly when you need him if he must be kept reminded constantly of the personal cost to him? Let us be as fair and generous in the practical items of religion as we would be in the successful conduct of our own business enterprises.

THE MINISTER AS EXECUTIVE

Third. A minister must be an *executive;* and here it is that we, as laymen, can help him most. He must be responsible for all three divisions of the work — preaching, pastoral and executive — but while you can neither preach nor enter into many of his sacred pastoral privileges, such as the sacraments of baptism and the holy communion, marrying the young, ministering to the sick, and burying the dead, you are peculiarly fitted by your own training and daily experience to relieve him of the business administration of the church.

This means, first of all, the maintenance and care of your church properties, including the parsonage. I believe that the house of God ought to be a shining example of good management to the community, with trees and shrubs and flowers and well kept lawns, roofs that never leak, walls that are decorated, pews, windows and equipment that are clean and in good repair. If you teach your children that " God is Love and Beauty " and that we should give our best to him, then let us first of all demonstrate our sincerity by making and keeping his house as beautiful as we can. This, of course, will be done under the direction of your trustees or house committee.

You, as layman, know well the rules of organization, advertising and publicity, investments and finance, campaigning and sales work, building construction, insurance and legal protection, accounting and office management, the conduct of business meetings, and the entertainment of conventions and conferences. In a sense of stewardship of your time and talents, then, carry these responsibilities for your minister and thus free him for the preaching and pastoral work for which he is so well fitted, but which you yourself can never hope to do.

THE MINISTER'S SALARY

One of your first duties is to pay the pastor's salary when it is due. I have known of churches which have borrowed from their minister, rather than from the bank, for meeting the current expenses of the church by withholding the minister's salary for months at a time. This simply means that the minister cannot pay his bills promptly, and the reputation of the whole church suffers as a consequence. In testimony of this point, I quote from a recent letter:

" I shall never forget the summer which I spent in a student pastorate, dodging behind doors to avoid my landlady, and walking in terror of the Chinese laundryman, because my salary had not been paid. As I was about to leave, a church fair was hastily organized, and my pockets were filled with the small change that was gathered in. They paid their debt to me except for thirty dollars, and the memory of those thirty pieces of silver still due me betrayed me into an attitude of mercenary resentment which clouded my future pastoral relationships. If the laymen want the pure gospel, free from worry and distortion, proclaimed from the pulpit, let them be prompt with the payment of the minister's salary."

Trust funds of the church should be kept intact for the purposes intended by the givers. The treasurer should be bonded, and his books should be audited frequently enough by a proper committee to insure public confidence. He should issue financial reports whenever they are needed by the trustees or the pastor, and money given for benevolences should not be borrowed for current expenses. How can a minister stand up courageously and make a report before his state or national board when he knows that his own officials are withholding for local expenses money that was pledged for the missionary program of the denomination?

Ministers should be insured against the uncertainties of old age. Their lives are spent in unselfish service, at nominal salaries, considering their training and abilities, and they are not in a position to lay aside funds sufficient for future security.

Some of the larger churches insure their pastor's life against accident, sickness or death, not only for his benefit but for their own as well, feeling that the loss of his leadership would be a financial calamity to the institution.

Every minister who gives the best years of his life to Christian service should receive the cooperation of the church in the payment of premiums to the retirement fund of the denomination he represents. All such items are justified in the regular current budget.

Frequently I am asked why it is that successful businessmen seem so unable to use their talents in the working program of the church. Many of them either try and give up, or do not try at all. They pay their membership dues as they would to a club; they attend services as they would a lodge meeting; but their patience gives out when it comes to organizing the various business committees of the church, or serving on their membership.

After wide observation and experience, I am convinced that the answer may be found in the fact that the basis of authority in business is quite different from that in the church. In business, we can say " Do this " or " Do that." We can use our telephones and order blanks, and press the buzzers at our desks. But in the work of the church, our only authority is that of recognized leadership. We can say

" Come " but we cannot say " Go." We can suggest, but we cannot command. And because human nature is what it is, our pride is often hurt, jealousies arise and our patience gives out.

But the voice of Jesus is speaking to us:

" Come unto me, all ye that are weary, and I will refresh you."

" Love your enemies."

" Do good to them that despitefully use you."

" Suffer the little children to come. . . ."

" Feed my lambs . . . and feed my sheep."

Jesus could not command his disciples, or even keep them from deserting him in the time of his greatest need, but because he loved them more than he did his own life, he won their everlasting friendship and loyalty. He taught them that only through humble service to others may the real rewards of life be found.

To your church there has been called one of God's true noblemen, to become your minister and your friend. You, as laymen, can either " make or break " him. You can criticize and humble him, or you can exalt him and give him unlimited courage for his tasks. He is sensitive, and he will respond quickly to what you expect of him. His ideals are of the highest, but in matters of business he needs your assistance. You ought to help him to grow in religious power, not only for the work of your local community, but for the interests of the church as a whole. His success depends, perhaps more than you realize, upon the help which you give him in the spirit that I have suggested.

Blessed is that minister whose laymen stand patiently and steadfastly behind him!